MARKED FOR LIFE

MARKED FOR LIFE
Prayer in the Easter Christ

Maria Boulding

First published 1979
Triangle edition 1985
New SPCK edition, with corrections, 1995
SPCK
Holy Trinity Church
Marylebone Road
London NW1 4DU

British Library Cataloguing-in-Publication Data
A catalogue record for this book is available from the
British Library

ISBN 0 281 04926 2

Printed in Great Britain by
Biddles Ltd., Guildford and King's Lynn

Contents

Acknowledgements

Thanks are due to the following for permission to quote from copyright sources:

Burns & Oates: *Greek Myths and Christian Mystery*, by Hugo Rahner (1957).

The Grail, England: *The Psalms, Singing* (Fontana Books 1966) William Collins Sons & Co. Ltd.

Dom Philip Jebb: unpublished poem.

Downside Review: 'Prayer and the Paschal Mystery', Vol 94, No. 317 (October 1976).

Faber & Faber Ltd: *Collected Poems, 1909–1962* by T. S. Eliot (1963); *Faber Book of Religious Verse*, Ed. Helen Gardner (1972). (U.S. rights by permission of Harcourt Brace Jovanovich, Inc.)

Victor Gollancz Ltd: *More Latin Lyrics, from Virgil to Milton*, by Helen Waddell, ed. by D. Felicitas Corrigan (1976). U.S. rights by permission of A. P. Watt Ltd.)

Excerpts from the English translation of the Roman Missal © 1973, International Committee on English in the Liturgy, Inc. All rights reserved.

Thames and Hudson Ltd: *The Way of Zen* by Alan Watts (1962). (U.S. right by permission of Pantheon Press, a Division of Random House, Inc.)

George Sassoon, Esq. and Faber & Faber Ltd: 'Faith Unfaithful' by Siegfried Sassoon in *Faber Book of Religious Verse*, ed. Helen Gardner (Faber & Faber 1972). (U.S. rights by permission of Viking Press.)

Biblical quotations from the Revised Standard Version (RSV) of the Bible, copyrighted 1946, 1952, © 1971, 1973 by the Division of Christian Education of the National Council of the Churches of Christ in the USA.

Biblical quotations from the Jerusalem Bible (JB), copyright © 1966 by Darton, Longman & Todd Ltd. and Doubleday & Company Inc.

Passages from Scripture, other than the psalms, are quoted from the Revised Standard Version, except in a few cases where the Jerusalem Bible has been used and the Sign (JB) is added in the notes. For the version of the psalms, see note 1 to Chapter 2, page 105.

Foreword to the New Edition

Adam has come back on to the cover of this book after an absence, and this delights me. Part of the beauty of the carving at Chartres is that it speaks of something unfinished, of work in progress. Adam is all of us, every man, woman and child, all humanity seen in the risen Christ; and God has not finished shaping his Adam.

In Christ himself the work is consummated; but it is characteristic of God's dealings with us that he looks for our collaboration. Christ's resurrection is a process; his body is the radiant nucleus of a healed, new-made world, in the building of which the contribution of each of us is needed. Adam sits there smiling; he still has everything to do in carrying out God's agenda, but as long as he stays in touch with God the work will be done, eventually.

Attunement to God in prayer is vital if our efforts and our energies are to be truly life-giving, if our cleverness is not to outstrip our wisdom, with the disastrous consequences we have already glimpsed. God calls people in many different walks of life to contemplative prayer. Yet to respond is to find yourself on no peak of serene wisdom, but rather in the heart of the Easter mystery, in weakness and hope, in the darkness and chaos of your unfinished self where, strangely, you find God. This is what contemplative prayer is about, much of the time. Many people today know this, yet sometimes need to be affirmed in what they know, as letters I have received since the first edition of this book testify. If the reissuing of it encourages you to believe in the call, and respond, it will have made its little contribution.

1 *Letting Go*

Whatever gain I had, I counted as loss for the sake of
Christ. . . . For his sake I have suffered the loss of all
things, and count them as refuse, in order that I may
gain Christ and be found in him . . . that I may know
him and the power of his resurrection, and may share
his sufferings, becoming like him in his death, that . . .
I may attain the resurrection from the dead. . . . I press
on to make it my own, because Christ Jesus has made
me his own.[1]

This book is about prayer, and primarily about the kind in
which the Christian engages when he is alone and silent. It
is not, however, much concerned with methods and techniques, except in passing, for there are many excellent books
on these, of which a few indications are given in the Appendix. It has grown from a twofold conviction: first, anyone
who seriously commits himself to this kind of prayer experiences its repercussions in every area of his life, so that it
becomes less and less possible to think about prayer divorced
from life as a whole; secondly, this pervasive experience is
an experience of death and resurrection which draws us
deeply into the Easter mystery of Christ.

Faith is a surrender of the whole human person to God
encountered and recognized, an act in which man worships
and obeys. The believer is called into a new life, but the
immediate condition is a letting-go of the old. The wrenching
away from 'what lies behind', of which St Paul speaks,[2] was
dramatic in his own case because he was the sort of person to
whom dramatic things tend to happen. In most believers it
is quieter, but equally real, and it is effected in a radical way
through the life of prayer. There is a death to be undergone.
Jesus stated this law of death and life very clearly: anyone

1

who tries to hold on to his own life will lose it; but anyone who lets it go for Jesus's sake will save it.[3]

Jesus demanded this because he obeyed the law himself in his passover through death to resurrection, and if we are to have fellowship with him we must go with him in his passover. It works out in him; it works out in Christian life and prayer; but it is also written across our whole experience of life and growth, for nature too obeys it in her own fashion.

The dying leaves of a hundred million autumns have built up the humus from which our crops spring, for nature had been practising organic farming for a long time before the mind of man was there to discover it. A hard, polished acorn falls to the ground and cracks open, but it sends one shoot down and another up, and later there is a tree. Life springs and grows where the bearers of life do not clutch it to themselves, but hear the call to let it go in the interests of fuller life and action. The caterpillar consents to the cocoon, sensing its destiny.

A baby may be really fast and efficient at crawling before he is prevailed upon to abandon it in favour of the precarious enterprise of walking upright. As he takes the risk he recapitulates the choice made by some of his distant primate ancestors. The adoption of an upright posture may have brought mechanical disadvantages to the evolving hominids who tried it, but with developing brain and keener sight, freed hands and tools at their command, they were on the road to civilization. The gain outweighed the loss.

In trivial matters and in greater we undergo the same creative discomfort. A person who has taught himself to type with one or two fingers suffers an initial loss of speed and accuracy when persuaded to learn the orthodox method, but the long-term result is greater freedom. The emotional and intellectual patterns of childhood disintegrate in adolescence, but the turmoil is the way through to fuller life. An association between two persons may develop to a point where rules learned in childhood about polite exchanges and letter-writing are no longer adequate; in friendship and love there are fewer signposts and a certain loss of security, but there will be great gain in humanity.

In most of these instances something has become as good as it can be at its own level: the baby's prowess in crawling, the adaptation of a species to its environment or Paul's Pharisaic service of God. The only way forward is a leap. If within our ordinary experience we know that by letting go of familiar living arrangements at one level we are sometimes reborn to fuller life at another, it should not surprise us to find that bewilderment, pain and the loss of our own tight control are part of the experience of being lifted by Christ into a life and love beyond our reach and understanding. In connection with the natural analogies just mentioned it is of interest to note that the Old Testament spoke of people who prayed as those who 'walked with God'; that Jesus compared himself to the wheat-grain that by falling into the earth and losing its solitary life is made fruitful beyond itself; and that he calls us his friends.

Jesus himself had to let go and leap. Throughout his earthly life he was in love with his Father's will, and though his obedience has many depths of meaning, it may be interpreted in the present context as a progressive liberation from all that was less than the Father's plans. There is plenty of evidence in the gospels that Jesus had from the first a consciousness both of his unique relationship to the Father and of his unique role in the establishment of God's reign among men. There is no need, however, to suppose that clear knowledge of the details of his vocation was immediately available to his human mind. It is not only that some gospel texts suggest his ignorance about certain things;[4] there is also the fact that ignorance about the future seems to be essential to finite freedom. If we always knew perfectly the outcome of our actions beforehand we should never have to take a risk, never step out into the open, never commit ourselves to an enterprise that may cost our all. There would be little room for courage or for growth. Ignorance is therefore not simply an imperfection; we need it in order to be human, and so surely did Jesus.

His human mind was real, and therefore limited. He inherited, as each of us does, a set of preconceptions, cultural forms and racial memories from his own people. He was conditioned, as each of us is, by his environment and by the expectations others had of him. His range of contacts was restricted. It is true that against this we must set the facts that a simple, uncluttered life, a good home, plenty of silence and closeness to soil and people make for clarity of judgement, and that his mind was not hampered by the effects of sin. Nevertheless his humanity was totally genuine, and among its ingredients was limitation, even in the matter of his expectations about his own life's work.

He had to grow from his culturally-conditioned ideas into complete freedom for the Father's plans, and he did so by obedience. The story of his temptations gives some insight into this process of self-transcendence, but his rejection of possible ways forward that were at variance with the Father's will cannot have been a once-for-all decision in his case any more than in ours. It may have become harder as he went on, especially when other people projected their expectations on to him; when he called Peter 'Satan' it was surely because a man who should have known better was doing the tempter's work.[5] It is difficult to walk the tightrope between really listening to others in order to value them and be open to God's word through them, and being so brainwashed by the opinions of others that we lose our hold on the truth we have glimpsed and are trying to respond to, a truth that is different from what the environment is transmitting.

Although Jesus must have freed himself progressively by obedience, it is possible that almost to the end he expected his Father to intervene in power. Gethsemane was the death-struggle between all that was less than his vocation, yet still had power to attract him, and the purer, freer will in him that could be content with nothing less than abandonment to the utter mysteriousness of the Father's love. He died in this abandonment, believing in the love of the Father who delivered him to death and seemed to be silent. His act of surrender as he said, 'Father, into thy hands I commit my spirit'[6] was the breakthrough, the leap beyond all limitations; such obedient love could be vindicated only on the other side of death. St Paul says that Christ was obedient unto death, but this inevitably meant obedient unto life: the unlimited life, love, freedom and joy of his resurrection.

This is what Christian obedience is about too, a stripping and freeing from all that is less than the perfect love for which we are destined, a means of growth towards the pure giving which is also the capacity to receive without any selfishness. The Church has always honoured the martyrs in a special way, because in them Christian sharing in Christ's passover becomes visible. Facing death and torture for their faith or conscience, many have found the strength to say, 'Father, into your hands I commit my spirit', and the Church has sung this verse in the liturgy of martyrs, celebrating a glory revealed. But many more have said it secretly, in a habitual radical obedience to God continually chosen anew. The glory is not revealed in us, but in Christ our passover is accomplished as obedient love becomes the heart of our life and, in a special way, of our prayer.

Anyone who prays knows the connection between obedience and prayer; between the 'Yes' which is expressed and to some extent diluted in the affairs of daily life and the 'Yes' spoken neat in prayer. We pray because we love, because we want to grow in friendship with God, because we want to give, because we want God totally. So if prayer is genuine and seeks God himself, rather than some idea of our own, it finds a need to incarnate itself in practical, daily aligning of our will with his. If there is a discrepancy between the protestations we make on our knees ('Thy will be done'; 'I want to want your will'; 'Whatever you say, I accept'; 'God, I want you and I don't want anything else') and the deliberate attitude of our will in daily life, our prayer goes hollow.

Although a little reflection and experience of prayer makes this clear, it is still difficult for us to let go of what we have or

5

think we have, of the immediate tangible good which to our caterpillar's-eye-view seems to offer life here and now. Obedience therefore has a death-like quality; it is a daily dying, a daily practice for that final 'Yes' of the whole man as he lets go of everything and gives his being into the hands of his Creator, gives without remainder at the moment of death. This unconditional surrender is something we secretly long for, try to make in prayer, and keep missing. We never seem to achieve it in an unqualified way, yet it is what we most want to do. The final yielding will be 'ecstatic' in the strict sense, a going forth from narrowness and ambiguities to the fullness of life and love in God. In Christ we shall say to the Father, 'Now I am coming to you',[7] and the committing of our spirit into his hands will be pure joy.

The rehearsals for it in obedience and prayer are commonly something less than ecstatic, but the fundamental will-act is the same. In Christ we say now, 'Father, into your hands I commit my spirit'; like Christ we often say it in pain and struggle, with no clear Friday-to-Sunday vision of the rebirth in glory.

> Mute, with signs I speak:
> Blind, by groping seek:
> Heed; yet nothing hear:
> Feel; find no one near.
>
> Deaf, eclipsed and dumb,
> Through this gloom I come
> On the time-path trod
> Toward ungranted God.
>
> Carnal, I can claim
> Only his known name
> Dying, can but be
> One with him in me.[8]

'One with him in me', this is the point. Obedience crystallized in prayer is not the imitation of a Christ-out-there, an attempt to model our attitudes on his in the way of people who are inspired by the example of a dead hero. There is nothing wrong with this notion except that it is insufficient. We can obey God because Christ's life, the Spirit-flooded life of his Easter, is in us; we have to let it spring up and do its job, which is to effect in us this leap into the Father's hands. In his act of dying Jesus 'gave up his spirit', John tells us;[9] the ambiguity is deliberate. He breathes forth his life, and when his side is open the water flows, symbolizing the gift of the Holy Spirit to the Church. In this Spirit of God we live our Easter life of grace and prayer. The fuller life is already ours since baptism, and it has the power to overcome what opposes it. When we obey God, therefore, we are not consenting to some requirement outside ourselves, but going with the pull of a life and love in our own deepest centre. 'For the love of Christ controls us, because we are convinced that one has died for all; therefore all have died. And he died for all, that those who live might live no longer for themselves but for him who for their sake died and was raised.'[10]

Yet there is more to be said even than this. Rising from the dead, Christ 'lives unto God', and we too are 'alive to God in Christ Jesus'.[11] Obedience is not an arbitrary arrangement imposed on us by God like the labours of Hercules, an obstacle race that we have to run in the hope of being crowned when we win through. Nor is it *only* a means of freeing us from our limited expectations, although this aspect has been a theme of the preceding pages. Christ's obedience is the human reflection of something in the life of God, and if we are to have fellowship with him we must share it.

John's gospel presents Jesus as the revelation of the glory of God. Its prologue says of the Word made flesh, 'We have beheld his glory, glory as of the only Son from the Father'.[12] This glory begins to break through at Cana when he makes the water into wine: 'This, the first of his signs, Jesus did at Cana in Galilee, and manifested his glory.'[13] The revelation continues in the subsequent signs, which present Jesus as the Life, the Light and the Love of God, but the glory shines through supremely in the final, single sign of his death–

resurrection. John speaks of this as an 'exaltation' which is accomplished in the hour of glory.[14] The whole of Chapters 13–20 in John's gospel are concerned with this glory: the humble act of service performed by Jesus in washing his disciples' feet and the supper-discourses which follow spell out the meaning of the passion and resurrection. The glory of God is revealed in the Son's obedience, in humble, unstinted loving-to-the-end.

Paul's teaching is similar. Writing to the Philippians he celebrated Christ's obedience in the well-known passage which is thought by many scholars to have been a Christian hymn already in existence:

Christ Jesus ... though he was in the form of God,
did not count equality with God a thing to be grasped,
but emptied himself,
taking the form of a servant, being born in the likeness of
    men.

And being found in human form
he humbled himself and became obedient unto death,
even death on a cross.
Therefore God has highly exalted him
and bestowed on him the name which is above every name,
that at the name of Jesus every knee should bow,
in heaven and on earth and under the earth,
and every tongue confess that Jesus Christ is Lord,
to the glory of God the Father.[15]

His incarnation was an act of humble self-emptying, and the obedience that led him 'unto death, even death on a cross', is vindicated in his exaltation. He receives as of right the holy name proper to God alone. There is a suggestion, therefore, that although Jesus consummated his obedient love in the conditions of a sinful world, the essential act at the heart of his obedience was a God-like act. This suggestion is clearer if we translate the first line not '*though* he was in the form of God', as most versions do, but '*because* he was in the form of God', which is possible. But the argument does not depend on this translation. It is the glory of God to give, holding nothing back.

Self-giving, self-emptying love, an ecstasy of unreserved giving in joy, is the inner life of the Trinity as Jesus has partially revealed it to us. He revealed it in his living and dying, but obscurely because of the conditions of the struggle. His obedience is the translation into human terms of a divine relationship; and moreover of a two-way relationship, for the Father gives and yields too, in delivering the beloved Son to death.[16] The other face of Jesus's obedience is seen in his resurrection: the life and joy and glory of God have transfigured his body and his human mind, but he is still the obedient Son. The act of giving is the same act, but what was painful obedience is now sheer joy. In the Entrance Song of the Roman Liturgy for Easter Sunday the Son speaks to the Father: 'I am risen and am still with you. . . . You laid your hand upon me . . . wonderful is your knowledge of me.'[17]

There is depth beyond depth in the dying cry: 'Father, into your hands I commit my spirit.' Jesus 'expires' and entrusts his last breath to the Father. He consummates his obedience in his act of dying and the cry marks the final yielding of his human spirit. His act of giving is an echo in the human world of the self-gift of Father to Son and Son to Father within their Trinitarian life, and this gift is the Holy Spirit. Finally, in Christ's passover to glory the Holy Spirit whom he eternally receives from the Father transfigures his manhood and is released to the Church. All these things belong to his paschal mystery.

We have to spell it out chronologically, but it is not simply a succession of events: first death, then resurrection and the giving of the Spirit. They interpenetrate all the time. In the dying of Jesus the glory of God is revealed, and the resurrection is only resurrection because it is the raising of the Crucified One, and the mystery of his loving obedience unto death is still there. A Christian who accepts the invitation to prayer follows him, for prayer is a process of being led by the Spirit into the paschal mystery. Yet even for us, immersed in the flux of history in a way no longer true of him, the

9

experience is not simply a chronological sequence. Death and resurrection, always interpenetrating, mark Christian life and Christian prayer. That is the central theme of this book.

The Lord Christ climbed on high
Above the stars....
Father, in this I have learned thy will,
And behold, I shall rise up at dawn.
Thou that dost hold me up, I shall no more be moved,
Receive me into thy glory.
Father, I shall praise thee for thou hast been my help:
And behold I shall stand beside thee in the morning.
For thou, Lord, art my helper,
And even now I am with thee in thy glory.

Son, thou wert always with me,
And all I have is thine.
Thou art exalted above the heavens,
And thy glory over all the earth.
Son, sit now on my right hand: return now on high.
It behoved thee, my Son, thus to suffer
And so to enter thy glory.

Father, thy word is truth.
Look upon the earth and fill it with thy good things.
Then shall I confess thee among the nations
And sing to thee in my glory.

Son, I have made her rivers drunk with wine,
I have multiplied the springing shoots,
And the fields shall be bursting with plenty
And the valleys thick with corn.
And they shall sing in glory.[18]

2 *The Hidden Easter*

You have entered with Christ into the secret life of God.

Prayer moves from knowing about God to knowing God; that is, to knowing him through the direct lines of communication he has provided: faith and charity. As this happens we move from comparative clarity into opaqueness, from some kind of feeling that we know where we are into a relationship where we have lost our bearings, and trusting love is the only way forward.

The strange thing is that though this kind of growth in prayer has been amply documented by the great Christian saints and mystics, especially St John of the Cross, it is still totally disconcerting. We do not feel that we have really yielded to God at all. Prayer is utterly obscure, but not in the way we expected it to be. We may have some theoretical knowledge of how it ought to develop, and even some idea of the progress of others if they talk to us about theirs, but absolutely no idea about ourselves: about whether we have even started, whether we have ever genuinely prayed at all. It is not just that we cannot plot our own position on the map of prayer that the mystics have drawn for us; the trouble is that we do not even know whether we are on the map. We read the mystics, the great classical writers on prayer, we see the vision of the heights, we long to go the whole way. We become familiar with the imagery: the dark night, the desert, the void, the cloud of unknowing, emptiness, abandonment, passivity, the cross. So in theory we expect all that. Yet we can still carry around inside us a secret load of guilt because in fact our prayer does not seem to be running true to type. We can have the sickening feeling that we are constantly failing, not just in this or that particular area of work or service, but right at the heart of things where it matters.

11

Possibly we are not giving enough weight to the fact that, by and large, the great classical writers on prayer had in view a public culturally somewhat different from ourselves. If you have been trained from childhood to use, develop and stretch your mind; if you have been pelted with huge quantities of literature and information and given jobs that demand of you a constant effort to enlarge your understanding; if your work-load is almost more than you feel you can carry, and life demands that you handle a good deal, cope, analyse, control, contribute and support, then it is hardly to be expected that when you go to your prayer you will always find it easy to switch from a busy mind with many thoughts to a still mind with one full intuitive act. It is possible that this typically modern experience of failure may be part of the plan, and that some demythologizing of the classical imagery may be useful.

We may find, for instance, that such images as deserts, dark nights and cross-bearing may sometimes be translated into terms like the following: 'I *never* succeed in balancing my life up properly between prayer (etc.) and work (etc.); I can't achieve a state of inner silence; I don't trust God enough to let go, or, if I do, I keep going back on it; he invites me to launch out into the deep, and I say yes, but then keep one foot on the bottom or swim back to shore; I can't quite believe, or anyway keep believing all the time, that he is keener on this prayer adventure than I am; I constantly fail to see that my whole set-up and everything in it is not merely tolerated by God (as though by a sort of half-hearted "permissive will"), but positively, lovingly, all-wisely planned and used by him; and—the worst betrayal of all—at times I think I have lost hope of ever arriving at contemplative union':

> Then they scorned the land of promise,
> they had no faith in his word.[1]

Discouragement is probably the most dangerous of all enemies for people who pray. In the seventeenth and eighteenth centuries, it seems, devout people were often tempted to think that God had reprobated them; presumably this was a trial allowed by God and a means by which he taught them to trust in his love. It does not appear to be a fashionable temptation today. In modern life discouragement more often takes the form of a conviction of spiritual failure, a feeling that all the pressures and circumstances of life are against us and are conspiring to block our progress towards contemplative union.

This kind of temptation is so common that it seems worth while to discuss briefly the problem of busyness in relation to prayer. In modern life most people, except the very young, the old and the sick, are under pressure. Clearly we must make time for prayer, do everything in our power to achieve balance in our lives and try to ensure the periods of rest and quiet that are needed for health of body and spirit; but reasonable measures of this kind do not simply eliminate the problem. The only ways in which we can protect ourselves from many demands are to refuse outright, or to fence ourselves round with the kind of attitude which makes it difficult for people to ask us to help. But these are not Christian options. We have no Christian alternatives to this exposure to life and people.

Because we ourselves are not omnipotent organizers and many of the given elements in our situation escape our control, because we are used to living with loose ends and rough edges and the partial disruption of plans, we can have the illusion that God too is thwarted by circumstances. But illusion it is: these circumstances, in all their seeming unsatisfactoriness, are precisely his will, and we must believe that he uses them lovingly and effectively for his purpose. It is not by getting rid of them that we are going to learn to pray and to progress towards union with God. The circumstances will block us only if we have not tried to make room in our lives for prayer, or if we think they are insuperable blocks (because this is to succumb to discouragement), or if we are busy for the wrong reasons.

A state of hyperactivity, if not due to illness, may be a shield against God, or an alibi from the more demanding task of waiting for him in prayer; it may be a seeking to make our own importance clear in the eyes of the others; it may be an attempt to justify our existence before God and other people, because we are afraid to be seen doing nothing. All these forms of busyness can be very considerable blocks to prayer. But the kind of busyness that results from generosity and approachability and being fully alive can be a modern form of desert. It can be a means of self-emptying in union with Christ, a purification and a true poverty of spirit.

'This is what the Lord asks of you,' says the prophet Micah, 'only this, to act justly, to love tenderly and to walk humbly with your God.'[2] The common experience of spiritual failure in the sense described can be a means used by the Lord to wean us from our own limited ideas about the way our life and prayer ought to go. We are forced to pray from a position of disillusion and bafflement, and this can lead us into the heart of Christ's paschal mystery. The real cross we are asked to accept is to believe that Jesus is Lord of every situation in our lives, and in particular that he is Lord of our prayer. From within our situation we have to listen to his word, and perhaps it may sometimes be asking us something like this:

'Do you imagine that my arm is shortened so that it cannot save? Do you imagine that because you do not happen to have a desert on your doorstep I cannot do in you what I did in the great contemplatives of the desert? Do you imagine that because I have given you a powerful and active intelligence and a job where you need to use it, the cloud of unknowing into which I am leading you could not take a special form? Do you really think that in this day and age when it is not usual to put wooden crosses on people's shoulders I cannot bring you into my experience of cross-bearing through asking you to live with tensions and putting on you a load of responsibilities you feel you cannot carry, or can only just carry? Or that I cannot lead you deeply into my own experience of utter smashing failure in Gethsemane and on Calvary? Do you really believe that your circumstances—circumstances not of your own choosing but largely shaped for you by your vocation—are going to thwart me in my plans for you? Have I been all this time with you, and you still don't understand? *Nothing* can separate you from my love or stop the work of my Spirit in you except your own deliberate and sustained refusal to trust me.'

There is a line in the psalms: 'To them he reveals his covenant'.[3] The Lord's friendship is for those who revere him, and to them he reveals his covenant. Jesus promised that the Spirit would lead us into all truth. We are not merely servants, but friends who are to some extent allowed behind the scenes. In the Easter mystery he lets us in on something of this bafflement we call our prayer.

In the gospel stories of the Lord's appearances after the resurrection there is a strange blend of familiarity and mystery. Jesus is simultaneously tender and mysterious. He is near and loving, yet not immediately recognized; playful even, yet awe-inspiring. He is with them, he eats with them and allows himself to be touched; and yet he says, 'Do not cling', or even disappears in the moment of recognition. Perhaps the most evocative statement is in the last chapter of John's gospel: after the miraculous catch of fish, after the beloved disciple has recognized him, after Peter has swum ashore to him, after Jesus has cooked breakfast for them, the evangelist reports, 'Jesus said to them, "Come and have breakfast." Now none of the disciples dared ask him, "Who are you?" They knew it was the Lord.'[4] They knew, and therefore they dared not ask. The logic is strange.

It is strange only because Jesus himself is in some way strange. He is not like Lazarus or the widow's son after their raising, because he has risen to the new, definitive, perfect life, totally transformed. He is very much more alive than we are. The new world, of which his risen body is the nucleus, transcends our world and is far more real.

St Paul tells us that in a way as yet imperfect, but none the less real, the same is true of us: 'You have died, and your life is hid with Christ in God. When Christ who is our life appears, then you also will appear with him in glory.'[5] This is said of Christian life as a whole, but it could be a description of the life of prayer. Prayer is a *hidden* life, not only in the sense that other people do not see your secret life of prayer with God, but in a much deeper sense. It is hidden from yourself. It is real, growing, human, divine life, but it is at once hidden and revealed under the sacramental signs of daily life, under scriptural word and Eucharist, under suffering and work and community and friendship and joy.

Even between human lovers there is a hiddenness, because another person is always mystery and the communion of love does not destroy it. The longest journey we ever make is the journey to the beloved person. A lover may know that there are no barriers, that he or she can be totally open and trusting, certain of being understood. Yet not only is there the irreducible otherness, there can also be a strange reluctance to speak directly about the love itself, about this wonder and glory that is between them; perhaps because it is too big, too holy, because they are afraid of spoiling or diminishing it, because they are wise enough to know that they should not analyse their joy.

Prayer is a journey to meet the absolute mysteriousness of God, the mysteriousness of his love for us and his action in us. As long as thoughts and words help us to meet him in a communion of love we should use them, but for very many people who pray regularly the point is soon reached when we sense that we can get closer to God without them. The real prayer goes on like an undercurrent, like something a person sees out of the corner of his eye without fully turning to look at it. There are moments in prayer when we do in some dim way know that we are responding to God without words or ideas or images, but if we turn to look at it or try to objectify it we are back in unknowing.

Prayer does, however, have certain perceptible effects. Although it is frequently humbling and unrewarding, we feel it to be of the utmost importance in our lives and are determined to stick to it at all costs. Further, the whole of life is simplified, which is not to say made easier. We have taken hold of something which pulls the diversified elements into unity; it is like grasping the knot underneath a child's toy roundabout and pulling the animals round the edge into their upright positions with one movement, or seeing iron filings align themselves with the magnetic field. There is an occasional intuition of the harmony and simplicity behind things, often in some ordinary domestic setting, and this is a touchstone of truth. We do not get more light in prayer, but we do perhaps get a certain sureness of touch.

This may be illustrated by a rough parable. Suppose you have to walk across a moor. You set out from a well-lighted house in which you have looked at maps and been given instructions. As you walk on, dusk is closing in and it becomes more difficult to see the way. Then it is completely dark. You cannot see your direction and it is so cloudy that you cannot even see whether you are still on the path. In fact, you cannot see whether there is a path, but you stumble on, hoping that you are going in the right direction. Then a thunderstorm comes on and the going is even rougher. But now and then there is a flash of lightning, and though it lasts for only a fraction of a second it is just long enough for you to see that your feet are on the track.

Something of this kind of experience seems to underlie the resurrection stories. Mary Magdalene outside the tomb is so near to Jesus that she could touch him. She has been conversing with angels and she even converses with the Lord. Yet she cannot recognize or understand; she is baffled and bewildered and the bottom has fallen out of her world. Jesus makes contact with one word, 'Mary'. Prayer is listening, listening to the word. Like Mary Magdalene we hear many words, but at rare intervals we hear the really piercing word, the word that affirms us in our being, the *fiat* that creates and re-creates us. This word is our own name. It is the secret name written on the white stone that no one knows except him who receives it,[6] the secret truth of our own person that we do not yet fully know ourselves but only glimpse, because it is only potentially true as yet, true to God but not yet fully brought to birth.

We identify very easily with the disciples in the resurrection stories. We are meant to, for these stories are not naïve reports of 'what happened'; they are written out of the faith and life of the Church as it experienced the presence of the risen Christ. We identify with Peter, looking into Christ's eyes on the night of his sin and so brought to his moment of truth, and looking into the same eyes after the resurrection for his forgiveness, healing and reaffirmation of love. The Emmaus story[7] is one of the best examples of all. Jesus is with the disciples all along the way, tender, encouraging, patient, loving, opening the scriptures. Yet they cannot realize it. They cannot see how the crashing failure could possibly be part of the plan. They voice their consternation and disillusionment: 'We had been hoping ... but now ...' It is the same with us and our spiritual programmes. The cross and the resurrection throw us into consternation and overturn our value-systems. We had hoped ... we had our plans about growth in prayer and holiness, but *now* ...! To us also the Lord says, How dense you are, how slow of heart! Ought not Christ ... and ought not you? Your plans were far too small and mean; let go of them.

3 The Battle of Death and Life

Mors et vita duello	When Death and Life contended
conflixere mirando;	the Lord of life was slain.
dux vitae mortuus,	A battle strangely ended:
regnat vivus.[1]	he won, and lives to reign.

The new life is already real in us, yet we still have a stake in this world which is groaning for its final redemption, and we groan along with it. In Christ death is defeated, but it still menaces us, and from its encroachments we suffer. It asserts its claim in advance over our bodies in the form of pain, disease, weakness or the process of ageing; it claims the people we love, with whom we have shared life and joy.

All loss is like a partial dying, and then our prayer is the prayer of pain and sorrow. It is important to let this be so. It is not truly Christian or human to be so bracing in our attitude to sorrow, whether our own or someone else's, that we try to supernaturalize it prematurely. To regard grief as somehow unworthy of a Christian who believes in the resurrection is to forget the example of Christ who was so often 'moved with compassion', who wept at his loss of Lazarus and prayed the longer in his own agony. We cannot short-circuit human processes; we have to give the experience time to come home to us before it can become a motive for hope and a promise of fuller life. Jesus told his disciples that their sorrow would be turned into joy, but he knew that they had to feel the parting first. Grief is only unchristian if it is wholly self-centred or if we never emerge from it. We always have to pray from where we are, not from where we or others imagine that we should be.[2]

Suffering strikes from without, but also from within. Not only is the incidence of mental illness and strain increasing in societies which are on the way to conquering much bodily disease, but everyone who lives life deeply goes through some kind of inner suffering. This is true of anyone who prays. For months or years God seems to be absent, and staying faithful to prayer is a matter of dogged, uninspired effort. The ancient and medieval writers on prayer spoke of *acedia* or accidie: the weariness, boredom, disgust and inner emptiness that beset nearly all at some periods in their life of prayer. It is death to joy and vision, at least on the level of perception. All through the Christian mystical tradition it has been recognized that this kind of experience is necessary, and usually repeatedly so, to purify the human spirit and prepare it for union with the Holy One, yet to know this is not to find the experience any less painful. Looking back, Israel knew that the desert experience of poverty, hardship and dependence on God had been vital and formative, but at the time it was thirst, rebellion, failure and sinfulness.

It is hard for a person in a time of accidie to know the difference between sin and suffering, because part of the suffering is the experience of sinfulness. This sinfulness is a state, not an act; it is radically different from sin because it is something we suffer and not something we do. Nevertheless it is bitter, and the state may feel like our own fault. It is, however, essential. The desert is not the desert unless it is too big for us; purification would almost cease to be a pain, and would not purify, if we could always clearly know it to be purification; life is not truly life until it has been menaced by death and come through.

My soul went waterless
over the harsh rocks,
down the dry valley of heedless stones.
Rough way,
and alone with darkness:
a tunnel to my tomb.
No tears to shed in that bleak world,
but only a stumbling on through desolation's symbols.

The first lift comes with the green fern
springing to the hint of light.

Then mist, and the rising water.
The boulders are rounded by the calling stream.
The falling path leaps to the sun.

Oh, glory of the day new found.[3]

The scriptures associate God's holiness and purifying action with fire: the Lord spoke to Moses from a bush on fire and cleansed Isaiah with a burning coal; the Spirit came upon the young Church in flaming tongues. We want God and all we know is fire, yet the pain is also a nearness of God, an inwardness and an action to which we can respond only by consenting to it in weakness. There are times when everything we touch seems to burn us, when we dimly know that God is at work and we can only stay in his hands, waiting for him. We learn a good deal at these times, even if we do not realize it until afterwards: 'Though the Lord give you the bread of adversity and the water of affliction, yet your Teacher will not hide himself any more, but your eyes shall see your Teacher. And your ears shall hear a word behind you, saying, "This is the way, walk in it", when you turn to the right or when you turn to the left.'[4]

Mercifully, it seems to be part of the rules that 'God always gives breathing-spaces'.[5] The battle between light and darkness, love and sin, life and death, is his quarrel and in the end will be his victory. 'The Lord will fight for you,' said Moses to the people, 'and you have only to be still.'[6]

In the Creed we profess that Christ 'descended into hell'; it is part of the Church's faith but we understand little of what it means. When we pray in darkness and anguish we may be touching the meaning. Christ has gone down to the roots of created being, and there is no darkness he has not reached. He walks through our hell; he is light in the dark places, life in the places of our death, love in the cellars of our hate. He has touched the roots of all our sin, and they wither. A branch may continue to put out shoots for a time after the root has been cut, but it is doomed. He is alive on the further side of death: 'I am the first and the last, and the living one; I died, and behold I am alive for evermore, and I have the keys of Death and Hades.'[7]

When we are in the desert and the death-valley, or have been, it is a mistake to think of 'getting back' to where we were before this pain came upon us, because we cannot be the same afterwards. It is a new thing on the further side. 'Remember not the former things, nor consider the things of old. Behold, I am doing a new thing.'[8] Pain is necessary for growth, the winter for the spring.

But there is a wrong kind of dying, for we can refuse to grow and cease to say 'Yes' to life at any age, and particularly when the *élan* of youth has slackened. In a marriage there is often a crisis when the last child is grown up and leaves home: the children have been the focus of the partners' love for so many years; the wife is losing her physical attractiveness; the husband may be past the peak of his career, and both of them look with panic to his retirement and the prospect of his being at home all the time. The only hope for them is to fall deeper in love, to say 'Yes' to this new phase together; otherwise there will be a slide towards negation, a shrinking of horizons, a shrivelling and hardening. This kind of choice confronts all of us at various times, whatever our vocation.

Amid the multiplicity of our existence, amid the activities and experiences and responsibilities, the issues come to stand out clearly. As God told Israel long ago that he was setting before them the way of life and the way of death, and they must 'choose life',[9] so we are called by the living God to 'choose life' and affirm it. Our society is afflicted by the threat of mass destruction and the temptation to deny life to the unborn and the aged, but there are also more subtle betrayals. It ought to be easy to accept the gift of life, yet we can choose to close in on ourselves and shut our hearts and minds; we can refuse the call to life; we can disparage, discourage and let something die. It is costly to affirm life always, for it can drag us away from our securities and threaten our comfort. Like the cigarette packets it can come with a warning: 'Living is dangerous to your health.' If we stop being on the side of love and life the pain may dwindle, because we are partly anaesthetized. But we are no longer really alive.

One of the effects of constant exposure to God in prayer is that we are 'marked for life': we are not allowed to settle for the pervasive withering of life, or to settle down in one corner of reality and make that the whole. 'It is a fearful thing to fall into the hands of the living God', says the Letter to the Hebrews,[10] but the comment has been made that it is far worse to fall out of them. In the end there can be no middle way: unless we mean to choose death finally and irrevocably we have no option but to assent to total, overflowing life with the living God. The assent begins now. If our prayer is an openness to God it is also an openness to his life, and the more we say 'Yes' to it the more it abounds, diversifies, enriches ourselves and others and enlivens everything else. The more there is, the more there will be. The more you give, the more you receive; the more you receive, the more you have to give. 'To him who has will more be given.'[11] Christ has told us, 'I came that they may have life, and have it abundantly'.[12]

In Istanbul in the little church of Kariye Camii there is an early fourteenth-century painting of the resurrection. According to Byzantine custom this is presented as a descent of Christ into the underworld. One of the most striking features of this beautiful work is the sense of rhythm and movement it conveys: Christ appears strong and active; with his right hand he grasps Adam's wrist and with his left Eve's, pulling them out of their graves. There is a vivid impression of dancing, as though he were drawing them into his dance of life.

'They shall feed along the ways, on all bare heights shall be their pasture,' says the Lord through a prophet, '. . . he who has pity on them will lead them, and by springs of water will guide them.'[13] A psalmist preferred to think in lowland terms: 'As they go through the Bitter Valley they make it a place of springs.'[14] There are many bare heights and bitter

23

valleys in the journey of prayer, but the springs of life are never withheld. Christ promised to give the Spirit as a leaping fountain: 'The water that I shall give him will become in him a spring of water welling up to eternal life. . . . If anyone thirst, let him come to me and drink. He who believes in me, as the scripture has said, "Out of his heart shall flow rivers of living water". Now this he said about the Spirit, which those who believed in him were to receive; for as yet the Spirit had not been given, because Jesus was not yet glorified.'[15] St Ignatius of Antioch in the early second century spoke of a living water in his heart whispering, 'Come to the Father'.[16]

We can draw water with buckets, or we can plunge into the river of life. If we are in, it is easier to pull others in, very much easier than trying to carry them to it across dry land. Ezekiel saw in his vision a river flowing from the new temple; he began to walk in it and it reached his ankles, then his knees, then his waist. Finally it became a deep and powerful torrent, bringing health and life to trees, fish, animals and men.[17] In the last book of the New Testament the same river of life is seen flowing from the throne of God and from the Lamb who was sacrificed and is risen:

> Then he showed me the river of the water of life, bright as crystal, flowing from the throne of God and of the Lamb . . . also, on either side of the river, the tree of life with its twelve kinds of fruit, yielding its fruit each month; and the leaves of the tree were for the healing of the nations.[18]

4 *The Real Relationship*

Like the empty sky it has no boundaries,
   Yet it is right in this place, ever profound and clear.
When you seek to know it, you cannot see it.
   You cannot take hold of it,
      but you cannot lose it.
In not being able to get it, you get it.
   When you are silent, it speaks;
      when you speak, it is silent.
The great gate is wide open to bestow alms,
      and no crowd is blocking the way.[1]

On the evening of the first Easter Sunday the disciples of
Jesus had locked themselves away from 'the Jews', their own
people, because they were afraid. Risen from the dead, Jesus
came through the barriers. He stood among them and communicated his joy, his life and his peace. The gift of his Easter
Spirit released them from fear, set them free for outgoing love
and created in them the will to give and share. He also
enabled them to live joyfully with the memory of their own
failure, because his forgiveness was a new creation in them,
greater and more wonderful than the first creation.

In prayer the barriers are down between us and God.
Jesus Christ comes into the prisons of our fear with the will to
set us free for love. Very many people are afraid—of pain, of
death, of loneliness and ultimately of non-meaning. The fear
of simply not mattering to anyone, of having no significance
and being unlovable, is one of the primary fears; it lies at the
root of much of the violence which brutalizes social and
international life. If meaning is thought to reside in having,
there will be violence on the part of both the have-nots who
try to take and the owners who try to defend their posses-
sions. Nations are prepared to take up arms to secure 'defens-

ible frontiers'. The same fear of worthlessness and unmeaning in oneself gives rise to ambition and competitiveness in personal relationships, and so to the petty violences we practise on others and ourselves.

Jesus Christ was fully and genuinely non-violent in his earthly life, not from any lack of courage to be otherwise, as he proved by his attitude to those in power, but because he knew his Father's love for him. Listening to this word of love, he had no need to grab at any possession or status-symbol. He could afford to be poor, open and gentle, because the relation of sonship was the whole meaning of his life, a meaning which unfolded through the years of his growing maturity to its consummation in his Easter. Fear he certainly knew, and for our eternal comfort he showed it, but in the moment of danger and abandonment by his friends his mind was anchored in the Father's love: 'The hour is coming, indeed it has come, when you will be scattered, every man to his home, and will leave me alone; yet I am not alone, for the Father is with me.'[2] The maturity of this trust was achieved through lifelong growth.

The Letter to the Hebrews says of Jesus, 'Although he was a Son, he learned obedience through what he suffered.'[3] If the New Testament had not said this first we should hardly have dared to. Obviously the learning was not a passage to obedience from disobedience, but a deepening and maturing in the human appropriation of his sonship. Son though he was, he had to work it out in fully human terms, and being human is not a static condition but a continuous growth through experience.

Human experience, particularly experience of relationships, interacts with prayer, and as this happens the person comes to understand and accept his identity. This must have been true even for Jesus. Although knowledge of his divine sonship was present from the first, it cannot have been there in a form immediately accessible to his human understanding; he must have needed time and human relationships before he fully grasped it as a man. The earliest and among the most formative of the relationships a person has is that with his parents. We know nothing of Jesus's home life except the brief indications in Luke's gospel, but his experience of the love he received from his mother and foster-father must have been powerful in the process by which he grew towards a human, existential knowledge of his Father's love for him.

Moreover, we know that he needed to pray; during his public life the need was often more imperative than the need to sleep. How he prayed we do not know, except that the word 'Abba' came readily.[4] But his human discovery of life, persons, relationships, joy and suffering must have been constantly interacting with his prayer. Being fully human he grew throughout his life, and his prayer must have grown with him, confronting him in his deepening human love and understanding with the Father's love and his own reality as Son. In mature freedom, fully trusting his Father, he went to the cross, and in his paschal mystery his sonship penetrated his whole humanity. His glorified manhood has so totally assimilated the Spirit of God that he becomes the source whence the Spirit is given to others. This Holy Spirit is the Father's breathing of love as he exults in his Son, and the Son's response to the Father. In pouring out the Spirit upon us the risen Christ lifts us into his sonship: 'Go to my brethren and say to them, I am ascending to my Father and your Father, to my God and your God.'[5]

The freedom that springs from the central certainty of being loved is part of the gift of sonship that he wills to share with us, and because it has the power to transfigure our entire humanity it must be progressive in us too. The long interplay of our very ordinary experience of life with our prayer draws us into the reality of our new being as children of God. We pray in the Easter Christ; whether we think of it in these terms or not, it is a fact. And so our prayer must in some way be a listening to the Father's word of love that gives us meaning and calls us into the freedom that is our birthright.

We can travel from our human experience to some knowledge of our Father. Parents love their child not because of some excellent performance but because to them he or she is 'mine'. They love him or her in a special way when the child is too young to achieve anything, or is ill, or handicapped. God can far more truly say of any one of us that he or she is 'mine'. We also know how in human relationships we can restrict people by not expecting them to be themselves, by labelling them and not believing the best of them. It is hard for me to be myself if someone has mean expectations that diminish me; but when someone expects very much of me, expects better things than I expect of myself, I instinctively know that this is a truer assessment. The best is the truest in the end; we know it in our hearts. The same holds for God, in both directions of the relationship. Because he knows everything in us he also knows us at our best, and in the warmth of his expectation we can grow towards it and fulfil his joy and ours. Conversely, by believing the highest and greatest of him we can remove some of the blocks to the action of his love in us, so that he can be what he wants to be in our lives.

In the parables Jesus turned to his own and his hearers' experience of human life, and especially of human relationships, to tell us what God is like. He pointed to the highest and best that we know. Human parents are sinful, yet they give good gifts to their children; how much more your Father in heaven. A boy squanders his inheritance, disgraces the family, is driven by starvation to seek a reconciliation without expecting more than a servant's status, and prepares a speech of apology in which he will outline his proposal. But his father has been watching the road in case some day, for whatever reason, his boy should ever want to come back. He cuts the speech short with kisses and exultant joy; nothing is too good because 'this, my son' is home again.

'No one knows the Father except the Son and any one to whom the Son chooses to reveal him.'[6] Though the Father is infinite mystery, the Son does so choose; the beloved Son whose place is in the Father's heart reveals him not only by teaching but by all he is and does. Here is another home-made parable. You are walking with friends on the flat roof-garden of a high building, engrossed in serious adult discussion. Near you a child is playing, a boy of about five. The child calls out to you repeatedly, but you are too busy to notice. Then he runs to the parapet, jumps on to it and stands there laughing, his back to the terrible drop. Your friends lunge forward, horrified, to seize him before he falls. But as you watch he laughs, waves and deliberately jumps off backwards. You do not share your friends' horrified reaction, because you know the secret: the boy's father is standing on scaffolding on the face of the building, out of your line of vision. Then the child is back on the roof, and he does it again and again, sometimes forwards, sometimes backwards, sometimes looking and sometimes blind, but always with delight. You never see the boy's father but you can guess a good deal of what he is like from the boy's relationship to him. You eventually want to play the game yourself.

By falling into his Father's hands, falling through death into his Easter life, Jesus shows us what the Father is like, but not only from the outside. He shares his own consciousness with us from within. In prayer I make the journey inwards, down to the centre of my own being. In peaceful attention I become aware of the inner unity of all that exists, of the loving energy that is at the heart of all creation and of my own consciousness. By discovering my own inwardness I am in communion with all other men and women, with nature and beauty and the goodness of all that is. Christ, the first-born of all creation, in whom and for whom all things are created, in whom they all hold together in their life and strength and beauty, dwells in the depths of my inner self. He lives in me, but he also invites me to live in him, to let go of what is mine and find my centre in him, where I am not lost but found. First-born of all creation, he is also first-born from the dead;[7] in consenting to be poor and losing my life I find it within his Easter life. He is the person in whom my personality is rooted and grows and finds fulfilment, yet he leads me onward to another. 'He who sees me sees him who sent me.'[8] The Father is in him and he is in the Father; his whole being as Son is a relationship, and his human consciousness is flooded with the glory of it. He wills to share this consciousness with us, to show us the Father, that we may share with him the glory and thanksgiving, the joy and peace of the return. This communion is the Spirit, their embrace and self-giving, the love and delight of their relationship, the dance of their inner life.[9] This torrent of God's joy is poured into our hearts, and in Jesus we are impelled to cry out, 'Abba'.

We do not know all this clearly in the time of prayer. We pray in faith and in darkness, and what awareness we have of the indwelling God is global and unanalysed. But it may help us if we know that our prayer is Trinitarian independently of any clear perception of ours. Whether we use the word 'Abba' or some other word or no words at all we are praying as God's children in the beloved Son, and the Spirit is shaping the authentic prayer of sonship in us at a level we cannot directly perceive or control.

The prior awareness of our new being in Christ gives meaning to our awareness of sin; the news of our sin would have been unbearable if we had not heard the good news first. It has been remarked that although the third chapter of Genesis gives an extremely vivid and perceptive account of Adam's revolt, and although the spread of sin and death is a motif of the following chapters, the Old Testament, for all its sensitivity to sin, does not develop any doctrine of mankind's solidarity with Adam. This is reserved to the New Testament. The Christ–Adam antithesis underlies the hymn of Philippians 2.5–11, often held to be pre-Pauline, but Paul in I Corinthians 15 and especially Romans 5 is the first to work it out fully. It seems that the development came so late because solidarity in sin would not have been intelligible except in the light of our solidarity with the Redeemer; the one was God's disposition in view of the other, and knowing it mankind can say, *'O felix culpa!'*[10]

'Where sin increased, grace abounded all the more', says Paul, 'so that, as sin reigned in death, grace also might reign through righteousness to eternal life through Jesus Christ our Lord.'[11] His perspective in this passage is universal; he is thinking not of the individual's personal sins but of the movement of redemptive history. Nevertheless, the same principle holds good for the personal sins by which we identify with and contribute to the sinfulness of the race.

Anyone who has ever made a sustained effort to pray regularly knows that there are two kinds of sin. First, there is a deliberate 'No' to God in any area of one's life, however seemingly trivial. This kind stops prayer until it is repented of. Second, there is the diffused but poignant experience of one's radical sinfulness, weakness, unfaithfulness and need of God's mercy. 'Feel sin a lump ... none other thing than thyself,' says *The Cloud of Unknowing*.[12] This kind is rather a help. I find at last that the rickety scaffolding on which I tried to stand has collapsed, and I am down on rock bottom. Since I cannot fall any farther there is a security about it, the security of truth. I am at last in my real and true relationship to God, a beggar at his door holding out an empty bowl, a sinner who has an indisputable claim on the one who is called Jesus because he came to save his people from their sins. I have attained to fellowship with the tax collector whose prayer, 'God, be merciful to me a sinner', was certified as genuine by the highest authority.[13] Moreover, since I can pray only from this position of a forgiven sinner, it becomes very clear what Christ meant when he said that willingness to forgive others for everything they have ever done to hurt me is a condition for prayer. We are all bankrupt together.

Repentance, or *metanoia*, in the life of prayer is therefore a moment of truth, a poverty of spirit and a stripping. All genuine encounter, and especially all deep human love, is something of a stripping; it forces me to let go of the little self-deceptions, of the habit of not looking straight at what is because I have been content with a stereotype, of the fear of seeing and accepting myself as I am. To pray is to risk this encounter with God and to stand in the truth before him. 'Everyone who is of the truth hears my voice', said Jesus to Pilate.[14] It is a summons on every level of experience.

Humility is not self-denigration, because that could be a lie. It is the steady willingness to stand in our own truth before God and to accept its consequences in life and relationships. Genuine humility can therefore be born only of prayer. It necessarily includes the recognition of God's gifts in us, since that is part of the truth, and a readiness to thank him for them, to rejoice in them and to use them freely when appropriate. So humility and compunction are on the side of life and growth and joy. 'The truth will make you free', Christ promised.[15] We are set free to love and we dare to be known. T. S. Eliot remarked that 'human kind cannot bear very much reality'.[16] We could not bear to stand in the truth of our being before God unless we first knew his love for us. In the certainty that he, wholly knowing us, accepts us, we can accept ourselves.

Only when we know that we have not the faintest right to it can we be truly vulnerable to God's love. Without this experience there can be layers of insulation, a defence, an insurance policy against God, a tinge of Pharisaism that tries to keep the relationship on a level that we can ourselves control: I have kept the law, so God cannot touch me; I am safe against God. To hit the bottom and at the same time know ourselves loved is to know that we are loved for no achievement, on no title, but gratis, for no reason except that God is like that and we are his. Through the prophets he used the tenderest language of human love to make us understand this: 'How can I give you up? . . . My heart recoils within me, my compassion grows warm and tender . . . for I am God and not man. . . . I have called you by name, you are mine. . . . Can a woman forget her sucking child, that she should have no compassion on the son of her womb? Even these may forget, yet I will not forget you. Behold, I have graven you on the palms of my hands.'[17]

It is true that 'God made us for his glory', but he loves us for our sake too, in the sense that, creating us, he truly wants us to be and wants our happiness with the whole force of his love. Our reality and consistency in his sight are not in competition with his glory, as though he were a little less God because I am I. He wants me to be me and to be most fully and truly myself, which I can be only when truthfully related to him. To know that I am unconditionally loved is the ultimate freedom. Things stand thus between me and my Father.

If you have known, even fleetingly, that Christ is calling you into this sharing of his experience of trust, it is vital that you plunge deeper into prayer, and give up trying to run it yourself. Hand over the controls and let Christ pray in you, and stop interfering with his prayer. You will not feel that things are going well; it will usually get out of control; it will leave you feeling out of your depth and wondering whether it really was prayer at all. Trust your Father enough not to worry about it, and ask for no reassurance. Have done with the works of the law and a do-it-yourself salvation. Pray in the Spirit.

Prayer may then become less an effort to love God and more a matter of letting him love you. Relax, because he loves you.[18] To be preoccupied with your unworthiness is not only pointless but obstructive. It is very humbling to be loved by someone who knows everything and still loves you, as Peter discovered on the lakeside after the resurrection. The love that knows us is creative, and so to let ourselves be known and loved in prayer is to allow ourselves to be changed. The heart of *metanoia* is not a striving to repudiate old attitudes and acquire new ones (though good-willed effort on our part is also required) but an openness to the re-creative love that makes the mind of Christ grow in us. It can therefore never be too late.

> The love that we have wasted,
> O God of love, renew.[19]

It will be joy to be judged by God in the end, if we have stood under his gaze, as far as we can, in prayer now. The Letter to the Hebrews gives a picture of all creation standing under it: 'The word of God is living and active, sharper than any two-edged sword, piercing to the division of soul and spirit, of joints and marrow, and discerning the thoughts and intentions of the heart. And before him no creature is hidden, but all are open and laid bare to the eyes of him with whom we have to do.'[20] Only at first sight is this terrifying, for the judge is the one who because he loves us knows us far more truly than any human judge and more truly than we can know ourselves. The creature desires, in the end, to be wholly transparent to God; it is the ultimate freedom and joy to be so known.

> O Lord, you search me and you know me,
> you know my resting and my rising ...
> You mark when I walk or lie down,
> all my ways lie open to you ...
> Behind and before you besiege me,
> your hand ever laid upon me ...
> O where can I go from your spirit,
> or where can I flee from your face?
> If I climb the heavens, you are there.
> If I lie in the grave, you are there.
> If I take the wings of the dawn
> and dwell at the sea's furthest end,
> even there your hand would lead me,
> your right hand would hold me fast ...
> For it was you who created my being,
> knit me together in my mother's womb.
> I thank you for the wonder of my being,
> for the wonders of all your creation.[21]

5 *Freedom to Ask*

Christ has become a priest ... by the power of an indestructible life.... He holds his priesthood permanently, because he continues for ever. Consequently he is able for all time to save those who draw near to God through him, since he always lives to make intercession for them.[1]

Being free in his presence it is normal that we should ask God about our needs and those of others. For many people prayer of petition or intercession is the earliest form practised, and it was prominent in the Old Testament. The psalmists cried out to God in any need, personal or national, and were uninhibited about material requests. So far from becoming obsolete in the New Testament, petitionary prayer takes on a more urgent and confident note. We can never leave it behind until the prayer is answered with which the New Testament closes: 'Come, Lord Jesus.'

Old Testament tradition believed that the prayer of God's special friends on behalf of others was weighty. Abraham had pleaded with him to spare Sodom, beating down the required condition from fifty just men in the city to ten;[2] the story is archaic and somewhat reminiscent of bargaining in a market, but the message is clear. Intercession came to be regarded as part of the vocation of a prophet. Moses pleaded with the Lord on behalf of his sister Miriam when she was struck with leprosy,[3] and repeatedly interceded for the people when by lack of faith and murmuring against the Lord they had deserved condemnation.[4] While Israel fought Amalek, Moses prayed on the mountain with his hands raised; when weariness overcame him he needed the support of his friends but prayed still.[5] Samuel and Jeremiah were later recognized as intercessors for the people in times of calamity.[6] Underlying all these stories is a conviction that the Lord wills to show mercy at the request of those who pray and live in intimacy with him.

Parallel to the tradition of prophetic intercession was that of atoning sacrifice. The priest also stood before God for the sake of the people, offering a complicated variety of sacrifices to expiate sin and bring the worshippers into a right relationship with God, so that peace and blessing might come to them. These two lines of tradition—prophetic prayer and priestly sacrifice—intersected at a vital point: in the Servant of the Lord.

This Servant, whose work and suffering are celebrated in four songs in the later part of the Book of Isaiah,[7] is a very mysterious figure. In the earlier songs he seems to have the characteristics of a prophet: he has been called by the Lord from his mother's womb; the Spirit of the Lord rests on him; he has a mission both to Israel and to the gentiles; his duty is to listen to the Lord and to speak his words; he meets with opposition as did many of the prophets. But in the fourth song he, though innocent, meets suffering and death on behalf of the guilty, freely giving his life as a sacrifice for sin and interceding for the transgressors.[8]

There are many theories about whom these poems had in view. The Servant is variously identified as a personification of Israel, as the prophet himself, or as some known historical figure. Whatever may be the truth about the immediate intention of the writer, Christian tradition has from New Testament times recognized that only in Christ himself did these prophecies find their fulfilment. Like the Servant, Christ 'committed no sin; no guile was found in his lips',[9] but 'he himself bore our sins in his body on the tree'[10] and by his wounds we are healed. He came 'not to be served but to serve, and to give his life as a ransom for many'.[11] He prayed at every turning-point in his life, for himself and for others, and on the cross interceded for his executioners: 'Father, forgive them; for they know not what they do.'[12]

Christ is both priest and prophet.[13] The efficacy of his atoning death and intercessory prayer is not limited by time or the conditions of mortality, but lifted to the heavenly sphere by his glorification. The Letter to the Hebrews, almost entirely concerned with Christ's priesthood, contrasts the impermanent character of the Old Testament priesthood and the repetitiveness of its sacrifices with Christ's eternal, efficacious priestly intercession in heaven. Yet an abiding element in it is his compassion for us in the weaknesses and temptations he also knew in the days of his flesh: 'He had to be made like his brothers, in every respect, so that he might become a merciful and faithful high priest in the service of God . . . For because he himself has suffered and been tempted, he is able to help those who are tempted. . . . For we have not a high priest who is unable to sympathize with our weaknesses, but one who in every respect has been tempted as we are, yet without sinning. Let us then with confidence draw near to the throne of grace, that we may receive mercy and find grace to help in time of need.'[14]

Paul's thought in his Letter to the Romans is similar: 'Who shall bring any charge against God's elect? It is God who justifies; who is to condemn? Is it Christ Jesus, who died, yes, who was raised from the dead, who is at the right hand of God, who indeed intercedes for us?'[15] In the seventeenth chapter of John's gospel Jesus speaks a long prayer of intercession, often referred to as his high-priestly prayer. It is attached by the evangelist to the supper-discourses and therefore appears to belong to the pre-Calvary history of Jesus, but its perspectives are those of his exaltation and the time of the Church.

It is characteristic of God's redeeming love that though Christ's work is totally sufficient, he should yet require us to contribute freely and lovingly, within the sphere of his grace; so Paul speaks of completing in his own flesh 'what is lacking in Christ's afflictions for the sake of his body, that is, the Church'.[16] The same is true for intercessory prayer. The sufficiency of Christ's intercession does not nullify ours or make it unnecessary, but charges ours with new power and meaning because it is lifted into his. A life of prayer in Christ places us firmly within the mystery of petition and intercession.

In itself this life of prayer in Christ is a mystery, not a problem, but it may be useful to clear the ground first by considering briefly a few of the problems it does raise.

There are the philosophical difficulties, much too complex to be discussed in detail here. The universe (so runs a common objection) is a closed coherent system of interlocking causes and effects. Any event within it can be adequately explained in terms of other events. Interference with these laws of nature is so repugnant to our reason that no alleged evidence for it could ever be admissible. Further, even if you believe in God, how can you suppose that your prayers change his plans? To these objections it may briefly be replied that not only is a fully deterministic view of nature less popular now than in the eighteenth and nineteenth centuries, but there is no contradiction between maintaining the rational coherence of the whole system as we know it and acknowledging a reality that transcends the system, being itself the source of the rationality and freedom we know within it. The Christian view presupposes a God who is personal and loving, and it does not think of prayer as an effort to wrest favours from him contrary to his prior intentions.

More real to most people who pray are the practical difficulties of coming to terms with intercession. Two are commonly experienced. First, there is that of walking the narrow ridge between, on the one hand, being so involved with the distress of others that we nearly bleed to death for them, which is not helpful; and, on the other, being inhumanly detached in a way that is insulting to those in pain. In practice we may find ourselves lurching between the two positions. There is no simple formula for keeping balance; but the more fully our prayer is made within Christ's, the more likely we are to share both in his compassion and in his joy. Second, there is the tension between the multiplicity of particular needs and the unity to which we are called in prayer. Both these difficulties belong to our earthly condition; they are two aspects of the same problem. The blessed see God face to face and all particular things in him; yet the author of the Letter to the Hebrews has given us the splendid picture of the saints as a great throng of witnesses watching us as we run our course in the stadium,[17] and it is not the habit of spectators at races to watch with polite indifference. The saints are presumably beyond the tensions we experience; in the fullness of love and vision they can care passionately for the details without losing unity or peace, because their love is like God's. We are still growing towards this reconciliation. Christ said to Julian of Norwich, 'I may make all things well: and I can make all things well: and I shall make all things well ... and thou shalt see thyself that all manner of things shall be well. ... I shall save my word in all things—I shall make all things well.'[18] We can believe it, but there is no short cut to this peace by simply bypassing the pain, and for the present we must live with the tensions.

This leads into the problems directly connected with faith and prayer. Some people say, 'I can't ask God for anything except himself'. Certainly this can be true at one level: when we are in prayer we may have to tread all particular thoughts and intentions down under a cloud of forgetting, as the author of *The Cloud of Unknowing* advises.[19] Words, images and awareness of particular needs are then a distraction from the dark formless love that brings us close to God. But the ample New Testament teaching on petition and intercession suggests that the inability to ask for particular things should not extend to the whole of one's life. Another problem arises from the early conditioning of those who have been taught from the cradle always to add a rider to any prayer of petition: 'Lord, let Mr Smith get better—but only if it is according to your will.' Obviously the ultimate submission to God's will is important in all we ask; common sense tells us that it is the only sane attitude, and we have Christ's example in Gethsemane: 'Nevertheless, not my will but thine be done.' It is possible, however, to abuse it, making it into an avenue of escape. If Mr Smith gets better, God has answered my prayer; if he dies, his recovery was evidently not God's will. Either way, I am covered. I do not have to go out on a limb in faith, I need not really commit myself, I do not have a risk looking a fool if my prayer is not granted. I have not had to wrestle with the mystery of God as Jacob wrestled.

The gospel teaching on intercession and petition is very stark when compared with these complicated problems. There are the direct injunctions of the Lord: Pray always; if you believed, you could ask for this mountain to fall into the sea and it would; ask the Lord of the harvest to send labourers; when you pray, say: Our Father, give us this day our daily bread; ask and you shall receive, seek and you shall find, knock and the door will be opened. Then there are the parables that illustrate the point: the widow who keeps pestering the judge to take up her case until he does so in sheer exasperation, and the man who knocks up his friend in the middle of the night.

Even more telling is the recurrent lesson of the way Jesus dealt with people in trouble. The wholeness of people mattered very much to him, and to set them free from their prisons of body and spirit was to effect in a visible and tangible way that liberation of all mankind which was the purpose of his mission. At the beginning of his ministry he claimed the Isaian text as his own programme:

The Spirit of the Lord is upon me,
because he has anointed me to preach good news to the poor.
He has sent me to proclaim release to the captives
and recovering of sight to the blind,
to set at liberty those who are oppressed ...[20]

His response to those who cried out to him in their need was to snatch the souls and bodies of the victims from the power of the 'strong man' whose grip he had come to break.[21] This was particularly clear in the case of exorcisms but also true of physical cures: 'Ought not this woman, a daughter of Abraham whom Satan bound for eighteen years, be loosed from this bond on the sabbath day?'[22] He obviously loved it when people flung themselves at him in their need, risking everything on his power and love, with no riders added to their requests: 'Lord, that I may see'; 'Lord, if you want to, you can make me clean'; 'If you can do anything, help us'; and so for the woman with the haemorrhage, the ten lepers and the Syrophoenician woman. There are no careful theological qualifications in their appeals, no hedging of bets. They take the risk of faith, they leap, they stake their all on his love and his will to save. They step out in faith, making fools of themselves in public. Sometimes it is more than one step that they have to take; the ten lepers were made clean *while they were on their way* to show themselves to the priests. While they were on their way! What if someone had stopped them and asked them where they were going? 'We're on our way to the priests, to show them that we've been healed'— and this while they were still covered with it. Peter too had to step out of the boat and begin walking before he found that the water would hold firm under his feet. The apostles had to start distributing the tiny stock of food to the multitude before they found that it would stretch. 'Whatever you ask in prayer, believe that you receive it.'[23] Otherwise you may not be fully open to the gift and able to claim it.

This faith is a gift from God, not a work of ours. We have a curious tendency to turn faith itself into a work that will earn salvation or the particular token of it for which we are praying. We think that if we can work up enough faith God will hear us; if he does not, it must be because the faith was sub-standard, so we must try harder. Of course it is true that faith does involve our free decision and that it can grow, but not by more straining. The good news is that God has already set us free; he has given us new birth in Christ who has already entered into the new life. 'He who believes in me will also do the works that I do; and greater works than these will he do, because I go to the Father.'[24] Faith is the fruit of the Spirit in us; he plunges us more and more deeply into the glorified Christ because he is the Spirit who cries, 'Abba!' in us, making us understand, though dimly, that our Father loves us and delights in us. Only through this work of the

Spirit can Jesus's trust and confidence, obedience and openness, be ours. Jesus gives us not only his body and blood; he gives us his mind and attitudes and outlook in the gift of his Easter Spirit. Only as the Spirit attunes us to Christ's desires can we ask the Father in his name. 'If you abide in me, and my words abide in you, ask whatever you will, and it shall be done for you.... Hitherto you have asked nothing in my name' (because they could not, until the Spirit of sonship had been given to form Christ's mind in them), but now, 'Ask, and you will receive, that your joy may be full.... I do not say to you that I shall pray the Father for you; for the Father himself loves you.'[25]

When the Spirit has free play in us we can ask and receive because the climate is right. At Nazareth Jesus was unable to work any miracles[26] because in an atmosphere of unbelief they would have been meaningless, just as the cures he did perform were meaningless in the eyes of the Pharisees. Miracles can be part of the normal run of things when man is in the right relation to God, a relation of obedient love and sonship; whatever consistency there is in the material universe is part of a larger consistency, and the source of the ultimate consistency and regularity of nature is to be sought in the character of a personal God, of which the material realm is a partial manifestation.[27]

Part of the Spirit's gift is discernment. If we are to pray for ourselves and others according to the mind of Christ we need to be led by the Spirit to know what to pray for and how and when. Jesus too had to pray for discernment; his mind was subjected to the Spirit not automatically but through prayer. He needed to soak himself in the Father's presence and sensitize himself to the Father's will. His night of vigil before choosing his apostles was surely not spent in focusing on any short list of candidates, but in a communion of love, trust and adoration that clarified his mind enough to permit him to take the next step in obedience.

In conforming our minds to the mind of Christ the Spirit also gives us the attitudes the Lord demanded if prayer is to be acceptable: total forgivingness, a spirit of repentance and unconditional trust. If we come before God to ask for healing for others, whether physical, mental or moral, whether individual or social, we must be prepared for the work to begin on ourselves: 'Heal my wife/husband, but change me first'; 'Heal that apparently impossible situation, but begin by clearing the blocks in me that prevent me from being an open channel for your power.' In attuning us to himself the Lord deepens our loving awareness of one another; when our relationships are right he can use us as channels for what he wants to give infinitely more than we can want to receive it. 'If two of you agree on earth about anything they ask, it will be done for them by my Father in heaven. For where two or three are gathered in my name, there am I in the midst of them.'[28]

It is clear from this that we may have to keep on asking. The Lord does not have to be worn down by persistence, as the judge by the widow, but he may have to make us persevere for a long time because he is purifying, teaching and fashioning us until we are ready to receive or to be used. The repetitiveness in prayer which springs from anxiety and is unworthy of God's children[29] is very different from the trustful perseverance he asks for, just as a 'couldn't-careless', opting-out attitude is a counterfeit of abandonment, trust and surrender to God. Our freedom to ask the Father in Christ's name means caring, even passionate caring, for those for whom we pray, but it also enables us to let them go into the Father's hands, believing that he loves them more than we do. 'The highest prayer is to the goodness of God which cometh down to us, to the lowest part of our need.'[30]

6 *The Prayer of the Psalms*

When Israel was a child, I loved him,
and out of Egypt I called my son....
It was I who taught [him] to walk.[1]

Prayer is always wedded to experience. This is true not only in the life of an individual, but also in that of God's people. We experience God and his salvation in what happens to us; but our fathers have done so before us. We inherit a very long experience of God, and a long tradition of response to it in prayer.

The psalms were prayer in human words, in which a whole range of human experience of joy, suffering, sickness and pain, the rhythms of nature and life, national triumph and calamity, love and longing, were poured out before God.[2] But God's creative power stood behind the events through which the men and women of the Old Testament lived, and in which they experienced him. The story of his salvation effectively began when he made a passage for some runaway slaves through the sea to freedom, so that in the desert they might be born as a people and bound to him by covenant. The climax of the story was Jesus Christ's passage through death to the new birth of his resurrection, and the establishment in his blood of the new covenant of love between God and men. Each Christian is united with Christ's death as he passes through baptism from the slavery of sin to his new birth in Christ's Easter life. He enters sacramentally into the covenant, and in his Christian life and prayer he tries to live out the reality of what has been done under sacramental signs. The whole Church, dead and risen in Christ's passover, celebrating the Easter mystery in baptism and Eucharist, and experiencing it at work in human life, looks forward with longing to the final redemption as a cosmic new birth.

Between these different enactments of salvation there is much more than a fortuitous resemblance. The earlier experience is a rough draft, a plan which, though it will be scrapped later, is necessary to prepare for the real thing. The exodus from Egypt was a saving act of the God whose redemptive love is deployed throughout history, in rehearsals that have mediated his salvation at a level appropriate to the stage men have reached, and trained them for its achievement in Christ. Behind the history of redemption stands the one God who wills to save, and the continuity of his action is reflected by the continuity of his people. Now the psalms are the response of God's people to the experience of salvation, and it is these continuities in the history of God's dealings with us that give meaning to the use and re-use of the psalms at different levels of prayer down the ages.[3]

Yet as God's creative power stood behind the events, so also did it evoke the response. The psalms were not only human prayer; they were inspired prayer: not only Israel's response to God, but truly God's gift to Israel. He spoke his love, and taught his 'son' to speak.

Jesus Christ is the 'Word of Life', the Word of God made flesh; in Christ's whole humanity, his work and teaching and death and resurrection, God speaks his final word. It is the perfect self-revealing word of love, the word that is active and powerful to save. Nevertheless Christ, being truly man, is also responsible for our side of this encounter of love; he is mankind's perfect response of faith, obedience, trust, love and prayer. For centuries God had looked for a response from the people he had chosen and loved, from Israel his 'son', his covenanted people. It was never given perfectly until the beloved Son came to be the new Israel, to relive Israel's experience and make it his own, and to establish in his passover the new and eternal covenant of love.

The psalms had been waiting for him, and on his lips took on a new fullness of meaning that was not a setting aside of their original meaning but its authentic prolongation and fulfilment. His whole life and ministry were a response of sacrificial obedience to the Father's love, and the Letter to the Hebrews puts on Christ's lips the words of Psalm 40:

When Christ came into the world, he said,
'Sacrifices and offerings thou hast not desired,
but a body hast thou prepared for me;
in burnt offerings and sin offerings thou hast taken no
    pleasure.
Then I said, "Lo, I have come to do thy will, O God".'[4]

Like the pilgrims for centuries past Jesus 'set his face to go to Jerusalem'.[5] A thousand years before, David had conquered the pagan city and made it not only his civil and military capital but the holy city of the covenant–God. To Zion he had brought the ark of the covenant, which had been like a sacrament of God's presence among his people. There David's son Solomon had built the temple where God promised to dwell, to hear the prayers of his people and to pour out on them his blessings. All through the vicissitudes of subsequent history, Jerusalem with its temple had been one of the great archetypes in the people's memory, a sign of salvation like the exodus and the promised land. Yet as Jesus drew near to the city he wept over its ingratitude and impending ruin.[6] The salvation for which it had waited was to be accomplished in it, but unrecognized; the passover that fulfilled all the old passovers would leave most of Israel behind.

In the gospel narratives of his passion the psalms are prominent. Part of the celebration of the passover supper consisted in the singing of the 'Hallel', and it is likely that Jesus observed this with his disciples on the night of his arrest.[7] But lines from various psalms are also used more personally. Jesus quotes at supper Psalm 41, the prayer of a man betrayed by his friend: 'He who ate my bread has turned against me.'[8] Similarly a line from the psalms is used to evoke the wanton hostility of the Jewish leaders: 'They hated me without cause.'[9] The Markan passion narrative records that Jesus cried out on the cross in the words of Psalm 22: 'My God, my God, why have you forsaken me?'[10] This psalm is one of the greatest and most poignant cries of the poor and suffering that the Old Testament preserved. It depicts an extremity of humiliation and loneliness:

> I am a worm and no man,
> the butt of men, laughing-stock of the people.
> All who see me deride me.
> They curl their lips, they toss their heads.
> 'He trusted in the Lord, let him save him;
> let him release him if this is his friend.'[11]

But it ends with triumphant assurance of the Lord's faithfulness and power to help:

> For he has never despised
> nor scorned the poverty of the poor.
> From him he has not hidden his face,
> but he heard the poor man when he cried.[12]

It is clear from all this that the shaping of the passion narrative was influenced by a realization on the part of the first generation of Christians that the psalms like the rest of scripture pointed to Christ, and that these things happened 'according to the scriptures'. They remembered the details of Jesus's agony in terms that recalled the great psalms of suffering:

> They tear holes in my hands and my feet
> and lay me in the dust of death....
> These people stare at me and gloat;
> they divide my clothing among them.
> They cast lots for my robe....[13]

> In my thirst they gave me vinegar to drink....[14]

John's passion account ends with the story of the piercing of Jesus's side, which the evangelist saw as a fulfilment of the prophecy of scripture: 'Not one of his bones shall be broken.' This is a double allusion: to Psalm 34.20 where the reference is to Yahweh's deliverance of the just man who trusts him, and to the ceremony concerning the paschal lamb prescribed in the twelfth chapter of Exodus. Jesus is the fulfilment of both types.

When he entered human history Christ entered fully into the experience and the memories of his own people, and when in his agony he made the psalms of suffering his own, particularly Psalm 22, he gathered up the cries of afflicted Israel and afflicted mankind, the cries of the nameless poor and lonely and persecuted of every time and place. The gospel accounts of his passion are objective and restrained; they narrate the sequence of events but give little indication of the inner face of these events as he endured them. The prayer of the psalms gives some hint of the subjective side, and with justice the Church uses them in the liturgy of passiontide. In Luke's narrative of the passion Jesus dies with the words of Psalm 31 on his lips, but the appellation 'Lord' is significantly changed to Jesus's favourite mode of address: '*Father*, into your hands I commend my spirit.'[15]

When Jesus appeared to the eleven disciples in the upper room after his resurrection, Luke tells us, 'He said to them, "These are my words which I spoke to you, while I was still with you, that everything written about me in the law of Moses and the prophets and the psalms must be fulfilled." Then he opened their minds to understand the scriptures.'[16] The distinction, 'law, prophets and psalms', corresponds to the threefold division of the Hebrew Bible, so the third item, 'psalms', probably includes not only our Book of Psalms but all the wisdom writings. Nevertheless the psalms are part of that prophecy of Christ to which he opened the Church's understanding, and as we can join the suffering Christ in praying them, so also can we join the glorified Christ who gives thanks to his Father in his resurrection:

> I was thrust, thrust down and falling
> but the Lord was my helper....
> The Lord's right hand has triumphed;
> his right hand raised me up.

The Lord's right hand has triumphed;
I shall not die, I shall live
and recount his deeds....
The stone which the builders rejected
has become the corner stone....[17]

My heart is ready, O God,
my heart is ready.
I will sing, I will sing your praise.
Awake, my soul,
awake, lyre and harp,
I will awake the dawn.

I will thank you, Lord, among the peoples,
among the nations I will praise you....[18]

Into Christ's triumphant thanksgiving is gathered the
thankfulness of all the poor and afflicted who have found in
God their refuge, and all of us who know something of the joy
of his salvation. The Church has prayed the psalms with
Christ down the ages, and as we pray them we are linking up
with something much greater, more continuous and more
powerful than our own private efforts. St Augustine says on
this subject:

God has willed that his Word, through whom he created
all things, should be our head, and has joined us to him as
his members, so that he, the Saviour of his body, may pray
for us and in us, and may be prayed to by us. He prays for
us as our priest; he prays in us as our head; we pray to him
as our God. Let us recognize our voice in his, and his in our
own.

When something is said of our Lord Jesus Christ which
implies some humiliation unworthy of God, let us not
shrink from attributing it to him, since he did not shrink
from sharing our lot.... He whom we have contemplated
in the form of God took the form of a servant, being born in
the likeness of men. He humbled himself and became
obedient unto death, and hanging on the cross he willed to
make these words of a psalm his own, 'My God, my God,

why have you forsaken me?' Thus we pray to him who is in the form of God and he prays in the form of a servant, for he who is the Creator ... assumed a created nature and made us into one single man with himself, head and members. We pray therefore to him, through him and in him; we speak with him and he speaks with us....

Let no one, then, on hearing the words of a psalm, say, 'This is not Christ praying', or again, 'This is not myself praying'. Rather let him be conscious that he is within Christ's body, and acknowledge both that 'Christ is speaking' and that 'I am speaking'. You must not say anything without him, and he says nothing without you.[19]

When Jesus died on Calvary the people of God died in him, to be reborn as the new people of God which is the body of Christ. The veil of the old temple was torn apart and a few years later the temple itself was destroyed, as Jesus had foretold. But his body, destroyed in his passion, was raised up[20] to be the new and eternal sanctuary of God's presence, the place of prayer and sacrifice and the meeting-place of men with God.

His Easter mystery was so radical a break that many of the psalms which the Church took over from the old Israel were at once transposed into a new key. The exodus from Egypt was a promise of the new exodus of Christ from the prison-house of death, and of the baptismal exodus of the Christian from the old sin-marked life to the new. The new people marches through the desert of this world, sustained by a better manna, heartened by the living waters of the Spirit, towards its heavenly homeland. The Songs of Zion celebrate both the reality of the Church on earth and the glorious city of God which will be the home of all the redeemed.

A sense of development and an ability to remain aware of different but interpenetrating levels of the mystery of salvation, together with a certain nimbleness of mind in moving from poetic, symbolic representation to actual experience, are a help towards making the psalms an expression of truly Christian prayer. This should be easier for us today who have come to think of man as essentially a historical being, one who grows and stretches out, with responsibility for where he stands now and for how he shapes his future by co-operating with God's shaping of it. Free movement between these different levels as we pray the psalms is something to which the Christian liturgy encourages us at the Eucharist and the great feasts. It is above all characteristic of the Vigil on Easter night, when Israel, Christ and Christian sacramental life are held together in one focus:

> This is our passover feast,
> when Christ, the true Lamb, is slain. . . .
> This is the night when first you saved our fathers:
> you freed the people of Israel from their slavery
> and led them dry-shod through the sea.
> This is the night when the pillar of fire
> destroyed the darkness of sin!
> This is the night when Christians everywhere,
> washed clean of sin
> and freed from all defilement,
> are restored to grace and grow together in holiness.
> This is the night when Jesus Christ
> broke the chains of death
> and rose triumphant from the grave. . . .[21]

A transposition most necessary for Christians is that of psalms where vengeance and the cursing of enemies are dominant. Whether the enemies were personal or national, the psalmists had no idea of loving them. They made an often facile identification of their own cause with Yahweh's cause; they took for granted barbaric practices common in the warfare of their day; they had no very developed expectation of a future life where accounts could be righted, and therefore assumed that, since Yahweh was just, justice must be seen to be done in this world. We can be aware of these facts, but simply to recognize that the crude vindictiveness of some psalms is typical of a more primitive stage of evolution will not suffice if we are to make these psalms viable as Christian prayer.[22]

51

The very ancient notion of the 'holy war' may be more helpful to us. All through the scriptures salvation is portrayed as a victory over the powers of death and darkness. The book of Exodus[23] describes the dramatic sequence of plagues as a battle between Yahweh and the false gods of Egypt: Yahweh performed his marvels through Moses, but the Egyptian sorcerers always matched them, and Pharaoh, hardening his heart, refused to let Israel go. On the night of Israel's escape the powerful armies of Egypt pursued their fleeing slaves. 'The Lord will fight for you,' said Moses to the people, 'and you have only to be still.'[24] As they stood on the further shore after the crossing, tradition had it that they sang the Lord's victory:

> I will sing to the Lord, glorious his triumph,
> horse and rider he has thrown into the sea![25]

After their desert wandering the promised land fell into Israelite hands because Yahweh continued to fight for them. Despite constant and terrible chastisement for their infidelities, they believed that Yahweh would always vindicate his own cause in the end. During the exile Second Isaiah represented the salvation for which Israel hoped in terms of the vanquishing of the gods of Babylon by Yahweh, the one God of all the earth. Apocalyptic writers down to Maccabean days continued to present salvation as the triumph of God's people, the 'saints of the Most High', over the great empires which had come to personify the powers of evil;[26] this tradition continued into the New Testament with the Book of Revelation. The coming of Christ was not an appeasement or a truce in the ancient warfare; Christ, 'the Lord, the mighty, the valiant, the Lord, the valiant in war', engaged Satan in the death-struggle of his passion: 'Now is the judgment of this world, now shall the ruler of this world be cast out.'[27]

Conquered by the Easter Christ, the powers of evil still have a grip on this world in so far as it has not yet accepted his lordship. The enemies who for the psalmists wore the masks of Egypt, Moab, Babylon or a man's treacherous neighbour are with us still: the sin in our own hearts and the sinful structures we have built into our society oppose Christ's cause. The warfare sung in the psalms was a primitive phase of a struggle between good and evil, love and hate, light and darkness, life and death, from which we have not yet emerged. Some of the psalmists' pleas are subchristian, but so are some elements within ourselves, for Christ is not yet Lord of everything in our own lives, and we all bear responsibility for 'the sin of the world'. As we pray the psalms of struggle we are implicitly saying, 'You can deal with all this. I can only come as I am. And I don't come alone; all these others are with me.' Further, though the outcome of the war is not in doubt, Christ has not yet claimed his cosmic victory. The Messiah for whose coming the psalmists prayed has come indeed, but we look for him to come again in glory.

There are, however, very many psalms where a radical transposition of meaning is not necessary; they are immediately viable as prayer at every stage of salvation, though Christians hear fuller resonances in them. The psalms speak of prayer itself and communion with God in terms of very simple human attitudes: prayer is listening,[28] thirsting,[29] longing for God,[30] waiting and watching for him like watchmen straining their eyes towards the place where dawn will break.[31] It is like the trust of a child asleep on its mother's breast,[32] like dwelling under the shadow of his wings,[33] like being embraced by him[34] and sharing his banquet.[35] It is even a life of weeping where God lovingly collects our tears in his bottle lest any be lost.[36]

The psalmists seem to have known something of that formless prayer in the dark where particular thoughts and images are not helpful but there is a dim sense of God's nearness and all we can do is let him act:

You hide them in the shelter of your presence....[37]

Of you my heart has spoken:
'Seek his face.'

It is your face, O Lord, that I seek;
hide not your face ...[38]

My soul yearns for you in the night,
my spirit within me keeps vigil for you....[39]

Be still and know that I am God.[40]

Contrition, poverty of spirit, experience of the human
condition and suffering at the encroachments of sin and
death give rise to piercing cries so elemental that they are as
appropriate to our situation as to that of the psalmists:

Make me walk in your truth, and teach me:
for you are God my saviour ...
Do not remember the sins of my youth.
In your love remember me ...
He guides the humble in the right path;
he teaches his way to the poor. ...
Lord, for the sake of your name
forgive my guilt; for it is great....
Turn to me and have mercy
for I am lonely and poor....
See my affliction and my toil,
and take all my sins away....[41]

A pure heart create for me, O God,
put a steadfast spirit within me.
Do not cast me away from your presence,
nor deprive me of your holy spirit....
My sacrifice, a contrite spirit.
A humbled, contrite heart you will not spurn.[42]

They know the alternation between joy in God's presence
and pain at the sense of his absence that is familiar to anyone
who prays:

I am like a dead man, forgotten,
like a thing thrown away....[43]

Your favour had set me on a mountain fastness,
then you hid your face and I was put to confusion ...

But then,

> For me you have changed my mourning into dancing,
> you removed my sackcloth and girdled me with joy ...[44]

Their life of prayer is a blend of delight and longing:

> O Lord, how precious is your love.
> My God, the sons of men ...
> feast on the riches of your house;
> they drink from the stream of your delight.
> In you is the source of life
> and in your light we see light.... [45]

But,

> O God, you are my God, for you I long;
> for you my soul is thirsting.
> My body pines for you
> like a dry, weary land without water.... [46]

They respond exultantly to the rhythms of the earth:

> The lands of sunrise and sunset
> you fill with your joy.
> You care for the earth, give it water,
> you fill it with riches.
> Your river in heaven brims over
> to provide its grain ...
> You drench its furrows,
> you level it, soften it with showers,
> you bless its growth.
> You crown the year with your goodness ...[47]

Those psalms which rejoice in creation are among the most immediately accessible to us; their pre-scientific framework of thought is scarcely a barrier. The universe revealed by modern science gives us even more reason to wonder than the psalmists had. The far greater stretches of time that we know to have been required for the emergence of the habitable earth and of man, and our relationship with earlier forms of life, give us reason to pray:

> O Lord, you have been our refuge
> from one generation to the next.
> Before the mountains were born
> or the earth or the world brought forth,
> you are God, without beginning or end. . . .[48]

> Already you knew my soul,
> my body held no secret from you
> when I was being fashioned in secret
> and moulded in the depths of the earth . . .[49]

One psalmist saw creation as an interlocking system of great beauty, a conspiracy of living things which serve each other's purposes:

> You make the clouds your chariot,
> you walk on the wings of the wind . . .
> You make springs gush forth in the valleys:
> they flow in between the hills.
> They give drink to all the beasts of the field;
> the wild-asses quench their thirst.
> On their banks dwell the birds of heaven;
> from the branches they sing their song. . . .
> When you spread the darkness it is night
> and all the beasts of the forest creep forth.
> The young lions roar for their prey
> and ask their food from God.[50]

All these creatures live and move and have their being because the breath or 'spirit' of God is in them. It could be withdrawn, but God can always re-create. This 104th psalm provides one of the best illustrations of the prolongation of the original meaning when the psalms are prayed in a Christian key:

> You hide your face, they are dismayed;
> you take back your spirit, they die,
> returning to the dust from which they came.
> You send forth your spirit, they are created;
> and you renew the face of the earth.[51]

A Christian can pray this only with awareness that the psalmist was saying more than he knew: he was saluting from afar the re-creative act of God in raising his Son from death and through him breathing upon men and nature the Spirit of the new creation. But the same is true, in their measure, of all the psalms; they are the dry bones of human experience vivified by the Spirit of God, and as the new things came to pass in Christ, and still come to pass, the psalms live again.

7 *Creation*

Spirit of God, on the waste and the darkness
hov'ring in power as creation began,
drawing forth beauty from clay and from chaos,
breathing God's life in the nostrils of man ...

Come and sow life in the waste of our being,
pray in us, form us as sons in the Son.
Open our hearts to yourself, mighty Spirit,
bear us to life in the Three who are One.[1]

The Spirit of God who is the spring of our prayer was revealed very gradually. In Hebrew as in Greek the same word does duty for 'wind', 'breath' and 'spirit', and these three ideas were not at first disentangled. The wind of God moved over the dark chaotic waters which in the Hebrew mind stood for the formless non-being that preceded God's creative act;[2] it is wind, scarcely yet 'Holy Spirit', but it suggests the power and mystery of creation, and it is closely associated with God's creative word. According to Genesis and the psalmist the breath of Yahweh filled all living beings, and in a special way it was the life-force in man: the human equation is dust plus the breath of God.[3] Without it there is inertia and death; so Ezekiel saw a vision of sinful Israel as a valley full of dry bones, but at the word of summons the wind-breath of the Lord blew into them; they were clothed in flesh and lived again.[4] The unpredictable 'Spirit of the Lord' came down as creative power and took possession of judges, kings and prophets, filling them with courage and vision to speak and act for the Lord.[5] Eventually this Spirit was to descend in fullness on the Messiah,[6] and through him to be given not only to a few privileged envoys but to all God's people. The Spirit would be like fertilizing rain in the desert,[7] creating a new heart in men and making them all prophets, witnesses and men of prayer.[8] Waiting Israel in the person of Mary stood open to the creative Spirit who formed the Lord's humanity.[9] He vivified that sacrificed humanity in the resurrection;[10] he baptized the new-born Church in power and formed it into the Body of Christ.[11]

Thus the Holy Spirit who is the intimacy and inwardness of God, who in prayer draws us to the roots of our own being in the divine life, is also the Spirit who makes it impossible for prayer to be solely inward-looking. To yield to his action is to be drawn into the creative, self-diffusive love of God, and so to be sent back again to all those beings among which his life and love are shared. The Spirit leads us into perpetual wonder at the huge array of God's creative ideas embodied in beings of all shapes and sizes and colours and aptitudes, with their ingenious methods of locomotion, feeding, fighting, reproducing themselves, caring for their young and simply enjoying their life. When to the contemporary spectacle is added what we know of earlier sports of creative joy now left behind in the evolutionary process, creation appears as a very surprising affair.[12]

There is an utter unexpectedness about God's creative act. Each time a new person comes into being there is a wholly new project, something never tried before: a new invention of love, a new way for Christ to be expressed in the world and a new sharer in the delight of the Trinity. It is not selfish for you to recognize the responsibility you have for developing this particular piece of God's creation which is yourself: body, spirit, person. No one else can co-operate with him at this point if you fail to, though others can help or hinder. It would be selfish only if you were intent on developing yourself without reference to the whole plan of divine and human love in which you are enmeshed.

God's creative power bears upon the creature not only at the moment when it is loved into existence but at every moment and in every dimension of its being. His power and love sustain it, giving it life and reality *now*. What this means for prayer is so deep as to be nearly inexpressible. I am here trying to pray, trying to attend lovingly to God, because I am alive and in love. And I am alive and in love precisely because his love is making me to be so; he has chosen the particular project that is myself in preference to unnumbered other possibilities; he has prepared my life through the unimaginable stretch of other beings in the creative process; he has given me life at a chosen moment and he holds me now in my knowing and loving response to him. Every fibre of my body and mind is shot through with this loving will of God that I should be, and, consequently, that I should now be before him attempting to pray. My very prayer is his creation in me, yet not less mine for that; rather more mine because his. My existence is his word of love; my createdness is itself a prayer if I have the wit to let it be.

More than that, it is in his own image that he has made and is still making me. When I look towards the Creator in prayer I know and am known, love and am loved, because I am like him. This is a fact far deeper than any perceptual awareness of it that I may happen to have. He has mirrored himself in the wonder of my being.

Moses said to the Lord, 'Show me your glory'.[13] He spoke for Israel, but also for the Greeks of classical and later times and for men and women of every age and culture who stretch beyond themselves towards a beauty ever ancient and ever new. 'You cannot see my face,' the Lord replied, 'for man shall not see me and live.'[14] So the Lord, we are told, sheltered Moses in a cleft of the rock, and shielded him with his hand against full exposure, and only some of the filtered glory was revealed to him. The Lord spoke to him in a cloud, the sign of his presence and mystery, yet the reflected glory on Moses's face when he emerged from the encounter was too bright for human eyes.[15] Jacob had had a similar encounter: he wrestled with someone in the darkness all night through, and his adversary vanished before dawn.[16] Not only is man incapable of seeing the glory of God directly, but God forbade his people to make images of him[17] lest their sense of his transcendence be dimmed and they fall into idolatry or magic. Yet God wills to be known, to show his beauty and share his joy.

One image of himself he did provide. 'God created man in his own image, in the image of God he created him.'[18] This God-like creature was intelligent and free and loving, the lord of the natural world:

> You have made him little less than a god;
> with glory and honour you crowned him,
> gave him power over the works of your hand,
> put all things under his feet.[19]

In the first chapter of Genesis God creates with a word, and man is his final artefact, made after the heavens and the earth, vegetation, fishes, birds and animals have been provided as his environment. The second chapter tells the story of creation differently: this is an earlier account, more picturesque and apparently more naïve, but of great power and beauty. Man is first on the scene this time, and God is a potter who moulds him: 'The Lord God formed man of dust from the ground, and breathed into his nostrils the breath of life; and man became a living being.'[20]

Neither account has anything to do with scientific description. Creation is the more glorious in our eyes now that we know that God did not produce things ready-made but empowered them to make themselves and transcend their origins, and that by these processes he created the mind of man with responsibility to shape the world. Both the Genesis stories, however, communicate in their own idiom the truth and reality of our relation to God as Creator, and their idiom has more to do with poetry and theology and prayer. In the north porch of the cathedral at Chartres are two carvings inspired by these creation stories. In the first God is creating the birds (his fifth day's work according to the schematic presentation of the first chapter of Genesis), but he is already seeing Adam in his thought. Adam's face, young and innocent, appears beside God's, and they are alike. And since God presumably does not intend to continue holding the bird he is forming, but is preparing to toss it free into the sun and wind, he cannot intend less for Adam who is of more value than many sparrows. In the second carving (reproduced on the cover of this book) the potter-God of Chapter 2 is at work on Adam's head, which rests on God's knees. With immense tenderness God shapes his image, and Adam, marked for life though as yet unfinished, smiles with such face as he has. In both carvings God's nimbus is cruciform, for the Father creates all things in his Word.[21] Yet the Adam of whom he is dreaming, the Adam he is moulding, is also to be in the fullness of time the man who is his incarnate Son.

Man lost the glory and the image was defaced. But the first creation was only Act I, only a prelude to the new creation in Christ. He was the Creator's dream all along; he is 'the image of the invisible God, the first-born of all creation; for in him all things were created, in heaven and on earth, visible and invisible ... all things were created through him and for him. He is before all things, and in him all things hold together.'[22] He is the new Adam, the fountain-head of life for the new race: 'Thus it is written, "The first Adam became a living being"; the last Adam became a life-giving spirit. ... The first man was from the earth, a man of dust; the second man is from heaven. ... Just as we have born the image of the man of dust, we shall also bear the image of the man from heaven.'[23] The contrast here is not only between the origin of the first Adam and that of the second, but also between their respective powers of transmitting life. The one lives because he receives divine breath; the other gives divine spirit. But while there is contrast, the law of solidarity holds; we bear the image of the first by right of common humanity, but we have an even stronger title to resemble the second.

We have known Christ only as Redeemer; the first-born of all creation is the one who is first-born from the dead.[24] Thinking on these things in a later letter to the Corinthians Paul explicitly linked together the Genesis account of creation, the glory of God revealed in the face of the risen Christ, and our experience of his death and resurrection in our life and prayer: '... the gospel of the glory of Christ, who is the likeness of God. ... For it is the God who said, "Let light shine out of darkness", who has shone in our hearts to give the light of the knowledge of the glory of God in the face of Christ. But we have this treasure in earthen vessels, to show that the transcendent power belongs to God and not to us. We are afflicted in every way ... always carrying in the body the death of Jesus, so that the life of Jesus may also be manifested in our bodies. For while we live we are always being given up to death for Jesus' sake, so that the life of Jesus may be manifested in our mortal flesh.'[25]

Paul was here speaking primarily of Christian life in general and of his apostolate, but this is a fair summary of what prayer is about. As the glory was dimmed for Moses by God's protective hand, so it is tempered for us by the humanity of Christ. But as we look at the risen Christ we catch the glory in our own faces, and as we are gradually assimilated to him we recover the lost image: 'We all ... beholding the glory of the Lord, are being changed into his likeness from one degree of glory to another.'[26] The Greek Christian Fathers spoke of this transformation as a deification, yet according to Paul there is no incompatibility between it and the experience of distress and weakness in our daily life.

When Jesus was transfigured in the presence of his three apostles he was seen to be accompanied by Moses and Elijah, the two Old Testament figures who had played essential roles in the covenant and who had come nearest to seeing the glory of God.[27] They spoke with him of his 'exodus',[28] and the cloud again signified God's presence. Although this occasion is the only one recorded in the gospels, and probably the only one on which the apostles were present, there is no reason to think that it was the only time that Jesus was transfigured. Transfiguration may have been something that often happened to him in prayer as he yielded himself body and spirit to the glory of God. Yet it was only an anticipation of the full release of that glory in his humanity, and on the recorded occasion it was directly linked with the approach of his passion.

Jesus's ordinary, everyday clothes shone, the clothes of work and sweat and travel; his ordinary body was transfigured, the body prone to weariness and pain and destined to suffer much more. The same is true for us in prayer. It is our everyday selves that are exposed to the transforming glory of God as we pray in the risen Christ, our weary bodies and our wavering minds, our failures and limitations and disappointments, our moments of vision and joy. Contemplative prayer is essentially ordinary for Christians. This is not to deny that it is the gift of God's grace, for our whole being in Christ is grace. It works out in great ordinariness, in the steady clinging of the will to someone we cannot see, and the humble, faithful effort to keep the imagination quiet enough not to interfere. When you are in darkness you may, like Jacob, be at grips with the one who has sought you out; when you are in the cloud of bafflement and unknowing you may, like Moses and the apostles, be very close to the transforming power of God. In gentle ordinariness Jesus says, Do not be afraid. You may have no direct awareness of the glory that overshadows you, but the transformation goes on without needing anything from you except consent. It may be also that outside prayer you are less inclined to look for the glory in the wrong places, and more apt to see it in everyday things and people.

When Jesus heals, whether in the New Testament or today, his work is a sign of that new creation so total in himself that not a razor-edge can intervene between the vivifying Spirit and responsive new-born humanity. The healings he performed during his earthly ministry were a first stirring of the new life among us, like the stray primrose that comes out on a mild day in winter, mistaking it for the spring.

John describes in the fifth chapter of his gospel the cure of a paralytic at the pool of Bethzatha: with a word and the man's (noticeably imperfect) response Jesus bypasses the supposedly healing action of the water. Challenged by the Jewish leaders because the cure had been performed on the sabbath, Jesus linked his work of healing with the Father's tireless activity in creation: 'My Father is working still, and I am working.'[29] He went on to speak of the Father's life-giving activity and his power to raise the dead;[30] the bodily cure is a sign of that present gift of new life for men's spirits which will issue in final resurrection for the body too. In his ninth chapter John describes the cure of the man born blind. Jesus heals him with clay (like the potter-God moulding man from it) and orders him to wash in a pool significantly called 'Sent', as Jesus himself was the one 'sent' by the Father for the work of the new creation. The man receives bodily sight and illumination of spirit; he sees and believes. The particular individual is also Everyman awakening to the light of the new day.

When Jesus puts his hands on blind eyes, deaf ears, bent backs, paralysed limbs, the Creator-God is at work through him, not merely patching up the rents in his old creation but really bringing in the new. It is true that the life he directly gives to broken bodies is natural life: the flesh that grows in leprous places will crumble one day and Lazarus will have to die again. But the Bible never makes a sharp division between physical and spiritual healing, any more than we can today with our awareness of our psychosomatic unity. When Christ heals, then and now, he heals the whole person, because the whole person stands open to God's re-creative power.

All this is implicit in the synoptics, explicit in John. Jesus heals with a word, as God said, 'Let there be light'; he heals with a touch, like the caress of the potter-God in the second creation story. Echoing the first chapter of Genesis John opens his gospel with 'In the beginning ...' and traces a pattern of seven days as Jesus enters on his ministry, reminiscent of the seven-day pattern of creation. At the end of the public life John again counts a week: on the sixth day the old order condemns Jesus and is itself condemned; on the seventh day Jesus rests after his work; on the eighth day the new time of the new creation is inaugurated in another garden. His resurrection is a greater birth than the first emergence of life. He spoke of his passion as a birth-labour that both he and his disciples would undergo, to be followed by a joy no one would take from them.[31]

In the obedience of his passion he laid himself wholly open to the Father's power and love, and his resurrection is the new creation revealed. With his scars still on him he came to seek his own and 'showed them his hands and his side. Then the disciples were glad when they saw the Lord'.[32] He gave them effective peace, wholeness. Then 'he breathed on them and said to them, "Receive the Holy Spirit. If you forgive the sins of any, they are forgiven".'[33] Over the new chaos that sin has made he breathes the Holy Spirit of the new creation, who is forgiveness and the power to forgive.

When we lay ourselves open to Christ's healing power now we are obeying his normal will that we should be whole. It is true that he demanded sacrifice and cross-bearing of his followers, but it is also true that the gospels record no instance where a sick person approached Jesus asking for healing only to be told that the sickness was a cross and he must get on with it. It may be for us the line of least resistance to assume that our infirmities are 'our cross'. Certainly this is sometimes the case, but it is also possible that they may be something the Lord wants to heal (perhaps through our vigorous and intelligent use of medical skills), and our reluctance to pray for healing may have more to do with unfaith than with acceptance of his plan for our lives. It takes courage to step out into the unknown like this, and our openness to his re-creative act may precisely be 'crucial'. In many of the cures recorded in the gospels Jesus waited for an explicit statement of faith and desire before he acted.

Behind the infirmities that we rightly or wrongly assume to be mainly physical there are the wounds that life has dealt all of us: the legacy of our own sins, of the traumatic experiences that were not our own fault, and of the confused episodes where we cannot separate the one from the other. Christ is not confined by time in the way that we are; he is the Lord of time and history, and so also of our personal history if we are prepared to let him be. Into all of it he can walk back with us, healing our memories and those forgotten wounds which have left us afraid. Not only does he forgive all that needs forgiveness; this we readily believe. He also enables us to forgive ourselves, a difficult thing for many people but necessary if we are to live as God's children. Moreover he empowers us to release one another, for we can all bind others by resentment and unwillingness to forgive. The Lord's gift on Easter Day was certainly the power of sacramental absolution, but there is no need to understand this narrowly. Sacraments are not isolated from the rest of life, but are the peak moments of our pervasive human and Christian experience. Christ heals now, as then, by using his body, and we are all his body.

For us, as for the sick and crippled in Galilee, healing spells freedom. The new freedom is ours, but we must claim it constantly. The Lord can, did and still does heal instantaneously when he wills, but he seems more often to do it gradually, whether it concerns body or spirit or both. A person may experience the healing power of the Lord in a clear-cut way at some important moment in his life, but this is never the end. He will become progressively aware of deeper needs, and will know that he is being invited to open these as well to the Lord's healing love. 'Behold, I stand at the door and knock; if any one hears my voice and opens the door, I will come in to him and eat with him, and he with me.'[34] We may think we opened the door to him long ago, but we live in immensely complicated houses, not one-room shacks.

From the experience of his re-creative love I can look back without pain, guilt or shame. I bear the scars still, but they are very different from wounds. Scars can be honourable tokens of battle[35] and of life fully lived. Jesus kept his and allowed the apostles to see and touch them; tradition says the body of the exalted and glorified Lord bears them for ever. Transfigured and glorious they are tokens of his love for us. The same is true of our own healed wounds; in heaven they will be glorious and the cause of more joy.[36] It begins to be true now, for I too am marked for life; my scars are tokens of his re-creative love, and as ever I must pray from where I am. My forgiven-ness and healed-ness are a prayer if I have the wit to let them be.

When memory has begun to be healed, it can do its work with immense significance for life and prayer.[37] St Augustine, believing on the authority of scripture that man is made in God's image, looked in the human soul for a trinity in unity, and found it in our memory, understanding and will.[38] Though man grows and changes, his life is not a cascade of unrelated experiences; the power to remember is part of the identity and continuity of the person and a means by which he comes to know God. The people of God has a long collective memory of all those events in which he has acted to save, revealing himself and his love. We call this long series of remembered events salvation-history; it forms the basis of the Church's response in prayer to the God who is present now in all he has done in the past.[39] But the same is true for the individual: you can look back on your personal salvation-history and recognize God's love in your life. This is the basis of friendship, for all friendship presupposes a history and some shared experience. To 'remember God' like this is a springboard for prayer. You know him because he has shown his love in your history; he is present to you now in all the reality of that love; you do not begin from scratch but take a great deal for granted because you are his friend, and you go on from there. When you meet him face to face he will be no stranger but the remembered Lover you have known obscurely all along the road.

8 Towards Wholeness

The Word of God,
born of David's line yet older than David,
disdaining lyre and harp, mindless instruments,
tuned the cosmos to himself by the Holy Spirit,
especially that tiny cosmos, man, mind and body.
On this many-voiced instrument he plays to God,
and sings to his instrument, man.
'You are a harp for me, a flute and a shrine':
a harp by your fine-strung harmony,
a flute by your breath,
a shrine by your reason.
Let the harp resound to his touch,
the flute breathe with his living Breath
and the shrine be a home for the Lord. . . .
A beautiful, breathing instrument has God fashioned
    man,
after his own image,
for divine Wisdom, the heavenly Logos, is himself God's
    instrument,
harmonious, apt for all melodies,
delicate and holy. . . .
What is it, his new song?
To shed light on blind eyes,
to open deaf ears,
to take the limping and the strays by the hand and lead
    them aright,
to stem corruption and conquer death,
to reconcile disobedient sons to their Father.
For God's instrument is in love with men.[1]

In the early years of the life of prayer many of us are somewhat individualistic and ultra-spiritual in outlook. It is not

that prayer is unrelated to life, but the life that has immediate bearing on prayer is mainly the moral and religious life of the individual. One of the paradoxes about growth in prayer is that while there is a deepening sense of personal sinfulness and inner poverty, there is at the same time an awareness of being led into broad places where some glimpse is given to us of the glory and vastness of God's work and of our human inheritance.

I may become more conscious of the great forces and movements that have shaped us: of creation and evolution, of the long climb to consciousness, of the earth and the seasons, the stars, the sun and the moon and our relation to these things. The megaliths and the ancient civilizations mean more to me. The huge adventure of the human spirit as it explores the cosmos and its own powers, the search for meaning, the creation of beauty, the widespread longing for a life that will cheat death, and man's encounter with God under a thousand names begin to touch my prayer in a new way.

This is not to say that I should habitually spend the time of prayer directly meditating upon these things. A prayerful person who 'walks in darkness and has no light, yet trusts in the name of the Lord and relies on his God'[2] may be closer to their centre and source. But in my prayer I am in some vital way related to them. In receiving life from God via my ancestors I have received so much. My small obscure prayer is part of something much bigger to which I am growing attuned, an ancient search for God that our race remembers.

From Genesis to the Book of Revelation men walk from darkness towards union with God who creates the light and in whom there is no darkness at all. After every night of affliction in which the believing watchmen strain their eyes for him, his salvation breaks like the dawn. God who on the first day of his work created the light and saw that it was good brings also the dawn of Easter Day, and in the end leads travellers to that city which has no need of sun or moon to shine upon it, being lit by the glory of God and of the Lamb.

In John's gospel this symbolism is very strong. The incarnation is the coming into the world of the Life that is the Light of men, the true Light that illumines every human being. The first gleams of his glory are seen at Cana. Nicodemus, not yet believing, comes to him in the night. Sinners prefer darkness to light, but the man born blind represents us all and comes to the light: 'One thing I know, that though I was blind, now I see.'[3] Darkness falls as the passion draws near, and Judas goes out from the light and love of the supper-room into the night. On Sunday morning Mary Magdalene comes to the tomb while it is still dark, and the gradual increase of light is paralleled by her recognition of the Lord.

In pagan antiquity religious men and women were fascinated by the sun. From Egyptian beliefs in a future life, associated with the night-travelling sun-barque, to Plato's cave in which men watch the shadows cast by the realities of that other world; from the Roman peasant's sun-worship to the Greek cult of Helios and the solar splendour of the Roman imperial religion, they saw in the sun the source of blessings and an intimation of immortal life. Christianity arrived with firm certainties: the sun was no god but a creature of the true God, and God had revealed himself not in timeless myths but in the life, death and resurrection of Jesus of Nazareth. These things being clear, however, Christians from the second century, and possibly even the first, appropriated the sun symbolism to express their own faith. Jesus rose on the day after the Jewish sabbath, the first day of the new week, and for Christians the first day of the new creation. This became 'the Lord's day' on which they celebrated the Eucharist and commemorated his resurrection; but it was also the day sacred to Helios in the Hellenistic world. On the first day of the seven, according to Genesis, God had separated light from darkness. The prophet Malachi had given the Lord's promise, 'For you who fear my name the sun of righteousness shall rise, with healing in its wings',[4] and Luke's gospel called Christ 'the rising Sun' from on high.[5]

People watched the sun sink in the west (where the gates of

Hades were believed to be) and reappear as a new, strong sun in the east; where he had been in the night or how he made the journey no one knew, but some thought he shone in the underworld. Christians watched too, and thought of the darkness that fell when Christ was crucified; his passion was a sunset and they believed that he had visited the underworld. He rose, a new, strong, victorious Helios, on the Sun-day, and when Christians celebrated their Easter on the holy night the candle stood for Christ-Helios. Buried with him in the baptismal waters they rose to the new life with him, and baptism was referred to very early as *phōtismos*, illumination.[6] In the rites immediately preceding baptism the catechumen faced westwards, towards the region of darkness, to renounce Satan, the lord of darkness; he then turned towards the east to make his profession of faith and commitment to Christ.[7] The 'orientation' of Christian churches was also common practice.

Christ died and rose in the spring, fulfilling the hope of the Jewish Passover feast which directly and primarily commemorated the exodus from Egypt. But behind the Passover stood ancient spring rituals, the sacrifice of spring lambs to ensure the fertility of the flock and the offering of the first sheaf of corn. Outside the chosen people the myths of death and rebirth were very powerful: the memories of the king who had to be sacrificed for the people, and the resurrection of the spring god as vegetation and crops were reborn after the death of winter. They were all vindicated in Christ's passover, those worshippers of Tammuz and Adonis and Osiris, the initiates of the mysteries that promised immortality, the Indo-Aryans who had rejoiced as Agni, their fire-god, sprang from the soft wood, and all those who through the ages had projected their hopes into the

> gods of unbearable beauty
> that broke the hearts of men.[8]

They are with us still, hiding in the shadows as we celebrate on Easter night with the new fire and the water, the bread and the wine, because no fragment of truth, no gleam of beauty, no act of heroism or kindness or prayer can be finally lost. In his earthly life Christ accepted cultural poverty; he was born into a race not noted for intellectual adventurousness or aesthetic sensitivity, and spent most of his days in an obscure village. It is true that Galilee was exposed to gentile influences, but on any reckoning his contacts with the world outside Judaism were very restricted. He lacked both the educational advantages and the experience of travel so formative in Paul's life only a few years later. Yet this poor man who accepted cultural narrowness is exalted as the Lord of history; all time belongs to him and all the ages:

> Ask and I shall bequeath you the nations,
> put the ends of the earth in your possession.[9]

In Rome the imperial sun-cult grew very strong in the third and fourth centuries A.D., including Constantine among its adherents prior to his conversion. Near the winter solstice the pagan festival of the Unconquered Sun was celebrated, and the Christian reaction to this led to the development of the winter light-feast of Christmas. The already prevalent idea of Christ's resurrection as a birth made it easier to extend the sun-symbolism to Christmas, and as Christianity spread northwards the magic of the winter feast became more and more powerful. Northern peoples had surrounded the ebb and flow of light and darkness with religious significance from prehistoric times; some of them have left a record of their beliefs and hopes in stone, notably in the megalithic circles at Stonehenge and Avebury in England and the chamber tombs at New Grange in Ireland. These megalithic monuments haunt our imagination still. Most of them were linked in some way with the sun's journey, and many were burial-places. Of the passage-grave type a marvellous example is found at Maes Howe in Orkney, where neolithic builders have left a burial chamber so designed that at sunset on the winter solstice (December 21) the sun for the only time in all the year shines through the long, low corridor and fleetingly touches the further wall of the chamber of death. The last beam of light on the shortest day glows for a moment on a wall that at all other times is dark. It is 'like a golden seed sown in the heart of darkness'.[10]

It was an easy further step to christen the ancient midsummer mythology that persisted well into the Middle Ages. John the Baptist's feast fell in June close to midsummer; he was not the Light, but only a witness to the Light, and he had said of Christ, 'He must increase, but I must decrease'.[11] So his feast, which marked the beginning of the sun's regression, reminded Christians of John's unselfishness, but below it is the ancient magic of the living earth: the short warm nights when the birds hardly sleep, when

> The Summer dark is but the dawn of day.
> The last of sunset fades into the morning;
> The morning calls you from the dark away,[12]

when our midsummer night's dream is very closely mingled with reality and some of us even in the space age suffer mild bouts of midsummer madness. Then as the summer months brought ripening, harvest and vintage, and the darkness closed in, the minds of Christians turned to another harvest beyond this present world which God is patiently gathering: the feast of All Saints in November promised abiding joy in Christ's salvation beyond the fluctuations of time.[13]

All these things still affect us very powerfully, and we should be less than human if our prayer were in no way responsive to them. Wholeness is to be found not in a strained effort to rise clear of the forces and rhythms that have formed us, but in accepting and integrating them. Prayer goes in wavy lines. This is part of the disconcertingness of it, because when we are in prayer and touching the simplicity and unity that underlie our life it seems as though we should be able to stay there always, as though we could never lose the truth in which we then stand. Peter's remark on the mountain of the Transfiguration suggests that he would have liked to make a permanent thing of it. Yet most of us swing between darkness and light, barrenness and fruiting-time.

Prayer is not a hobby but a life, and to live is to change. Human life is rhythmic: the body has its biological rhythms and its alternations between effort and rest, and on these are built the work-rhythms of our days and weeks, our term and vacation, our new drives and summer holidays. Women are especially susceptible to them, as when the primeval urge to spring-cleaning becomes irresistible. An urban way of life tends to mask the seasonal fluctuations,[14] but although in an agricultural economy they are more evident and inescapable, we all have to live rhythmically in some degree. 'While earth remains, seedtime and harvest, cold and heat, summer and winter, day and night, shall not cease.'[15] We shall be the poorer if we become such strangers to the earth that these changes no longer affect us, and the annual marvel of death and rebirth can no longer make us catch our breath.

Inevitably prayer will be like this too, since it is part of the plan of creation and redemption. You will know winter and spring, the disappointing gap when nothing seems to be happening between the glory of blossom-time and the appearance of the first tiny apples, and the deep peace of harvest. In other people at least, if not in yourself, you may see something like the tree which looks so ordinary all the year, but in the cold mists of autumn catches fire and is a blaze of glory for the few days before its leaves fall. Through the changes you must stick to prayer, regularly and hopefully, believing in the efficacious work that is going on in you.

For centuries the Christian tradition has been enriched by descriptions of the development of prayer left by the great writers of the Middle Ages and of the sixteenth and seventeenth centuries. The chronological schemes provided must not be interpreted over-rigidly; it can be said that this or that kind of prayer is typical of a certain stage but, since God is supremely free with his graces and the human material so varied, hard and fast delineations are out of place. It may be that we have fleeting foretastes of the final union long before we reach it, because we touch the mature Spirit dwelling and praying within us. Or it may be that growth in experience is more like climbing a spiral staircase: we go round and round, yet we are higher up each time, seeing the same landscape but with a longer view. Nevertheless there is a non-cyclic kind of change: the movement we cannot directly watch from youth to maturity, and the positive growth towards death; and this is necessarily reflected in our prayer. There is a sense in which we grow younger, grow in the capacity to wonder and enjoy, and find in ourselves a new simplicity and reconciliation as a fruit of persevering prayer. We become free to play in God's presence.

Play, like true culture, is not a means to an end, not utilitarian, but a human activity worth while in itself. It is the outflow of joy, skill and harmony, the expression of the spirit's mastery over the body's powers. Agility and grace, elegance and rhythm, the freedom of sheer enjoyment and the easy control of movement, gesture, sound, word or colour—all these speak of the wholeness which God meant to exist in us and which we shall find again. The ability to play before God and to dance in his presence is ours because we secretly know our kinship with a life and an order of being beyond the pains and labours of everyday existence; the person who plays or dances, hardly knowing why he does so, participates in the dance of all creation. In laughter we touch an eternal order of rightness and sanity.[16]

The myths spoke of a *puer aeternus*, an eternal child or child-god who plays for ever,[17] and this archetype so deep in our racial memory appears in the Old Testament too. When God conceived the glory of creation, his master-idea, his 'Wisdom', was like a joyful child, playing freely 'before his face', delighting in the loveliness of it all:

> When he fixed the heavens firm, I was there,
> when he drew a ring on the surface of the deep,
> when he assigned the sea its boundaries ...
> when he laid down the foundations of the earth,
> I was by his side, a master craftsman,
> delighting him day after day,
> ever at play in his presence,
> at play everywhere in his world.[18]

The author of the greatest creation psalm blessed God for the sea

> with its moving swarms past counting . . .
> and the monsters you made to play with.[19]

Even in the solemn confrontation between God and Job which forms the climax of one of the most profound books of the Old Testament there is the same playful delight in the giants of creation:

> Do you give the horse his might?
> Do you clothe his neck with strength? . . .
> His majestic snorting is terrible.
> He paws in the valley, and exults in his strength . . .
> With fierceness and rage he swallows the ground;
> he cannot stand still at the sound of the trumpet.
> When the trumpet sounds, he says 'Aha!'
> He smells the battle from afar . . .
>
> Behold Behemoth [the hippopotamus],
> which I made as I made you . . .
> Behold, his strength is in his loins,
> and his power in the muscles of his belly.
> He makes his tail stiff as a cedar;
> the sinews of his thighs are knit together.
> His bones are tubes of bronze
> his limbs like bars of iron.[20]

The stars, we are told in the Book of Baruch,

> shone in their watches and were glad;
> he called them, and they said, 'Here we are!'
> They shone with gladness for him who made them.[21]

No doubt he was pleased to be informed. There is a glorious lightness in all this that can only have come from the hearts of men at home in God's presence. One of the best examples of all is the whole of that gem called the Book of Jonah; throughout the book the humour and gentle playfulness of

Yahweh contrast with the tight-lipped harshness of his righteous prophet, and they take us close to the heart of God.

You may pray the better if you understand that the changes in your life of prayer are partly lover's play and the fortunes of the dance. You have to go with them, attuned to him and responding like a supple partner. To change the metaphor a little, you are a song God is singing; a song takes time and includes periods of silence, climax and quiet passages.[22] The Breath of the risen Christ is in you, and through you can awaken the song latent in all creatures.

9 *Pruning*

I am the true vine, and my Father is the vinedresser.
Every branch of mine that bears no fruit, he takes away,
and every branch that does bear fruit he prunes, that it
may bear more fruit. ... He who abides in me and I in
him, he it is that bears much fruit, for apart from me
you can do nothing. ... By this is my Father glorified,
that you bear much fruit.[1]

To allow God to play us and play with us, and to be prepared
to play with him, is to be close to the source of human
creativity. This is obvious in any form of artistic achievement, but creativity is much wider. You can live creatively.
Love is of its nature creative, and so is giving or increasing
life in any way, whether by parenthood, rearing children,
making a home, building up family or community life, teaching, healing, bringing order out of chaos, giving or making
peace, or enjoying friendship. God's creative power and
inspiration do not bypass our human processes. We still
bungle, make mistakes, sweat away at it, take it to pieces and
begin again, abandon the original plan and try another and
endure the pain of not being able to begin. Yet God fully uses
us, up to our human capacity, as we respond to him. As I
create something, laboriously and lovingly shaping it, God
is patiently and lovingly shaping me. Our work is within
his.[2]

Art feeds on sacrifice. To consent thus to live creatively
within our createdness is to accept, as every creator does, the
limitations inherent in the material or the chosen form: the
grain of the wood, the strict lines of the sonnet, the heart-
breaking task of pruning the young tree. Christ accepted the
very tight confines of his human career, its brevity and its
cultural poverty; within them he lived and died more crea-

tively than anyone has ever done. The hardest thing is to accept not only the limitations of the environment but the limitations in oneself. For a time, while I am young, facing my limitations is not imperative, because I can always tell myself that I have not yet had time to achieve my dream. Given time, I shall get there. But the day comes when I realize that I am never going to achieve it, because I am not the sort of person who can. The ideal means as much to me as ever, but my instrument will not play that note. It is a very painful realization, and much may depend on what I do with it. I can rebel and refuse to face it, which leads to resentment and a flirtation with unreality. I can acquiesce in a cynical and disillusioned way, which leads to loss of the vision and checks growth. Or I can accept it very lovingly in faith.

At a greater depth than before I am being asked to accept the reality of the human condition. God's Son accepted it in his incarnation more deeply and lovingly than I shall ever be able to, but my acceptance is within his. He did the Father's perfect work within his limited humanity, and all humanity's limitations are shot through with glory in consequence. God has chosen, freely chosen, to work creatively within my limitations too. When I accept them I am consenting to go along with his vision, not acquiescing in some kind of regretful decision on his part to make the best of a bad job.

Anything that is real and genuine in our vision will be found again later, but God has a greater vision and he has to prune away what hinders its realization. Through the failures, disappointments, humiliations and losses that diminish us he is pruning for the sake of fuller life, growth and fruitfulness. The only thing required of us is that we trust him and consent, and do not grow bitter. If we persevere in prayer we cannot escape pruning; if it is really God whom we encounter, self-sufficiency will not survive intact. Jacob wrestled alone in the dark with God, as does everyone committed to prayer; when he refused to let go his opponent touched his hip, and Jacob limped thereafter.[3] A man of prayer is marked for life in every sense.

Come, O thou Traveller unknown,
   Whom I still hold, but cannot see,
My company before is gone,
   And I am left alone with thee,
With thee all night I mean to stay,
And wrestle till the break of day.

I need not tell thee who I am,
   My misery, or sin declare,
Thyself hast called me by my name,
   Look on thy hands, and read it there,
But who, I ask thee, who art thou?
Tell me thy name, and tell me now....

What though my shrinking flesh complain,
   And murmur to contend so long,
I rise superior to my pain,
   When I am weak then I am strong,
And when my all of strength shall fail,
I shall with the God-Man prevail....

Yield to me now—for I am weak;
   But confident in self-despair:
Speak to my heart, in blessings speak,
   Be conquered by my instant prayer,
Speak, or thou never hence shall move,
And tell me, if thy name is Love....[4]

Creative living is also the fruit of tensions, tensions understood and accepted with love. The word 'tension' is frequently used pejoratively, but every creative thing that
happens in our experience is the outcome of some living
tension: male and female, solitude and community, professional involvement and family life, the boldness of the overall
plan and the perfection of the details. Christian hope is a
tension between the insecurity of one still on the way and the
certainty of God's faithfulness; prayer itself is a tension
between the not-yet and the already-given. In prayer we
grope our way towards the loving unity of which all these

good things in tension with each other are spin-offs; through prayer we learn to live with them lovingly and in peace.

Peace is quite compatible with felt tensions. The peace of Christ is his own gift: 'My peace I give to you; not as the world gives do I give to you.'[5] You do not generate it but you are asked to accept it, to live in it, walk in it, let him create it in you, and step back into it when you have fallen out. It is like accepting forgiveness and healing, a self-transcending act. Because this peace is an aspect of the new Easter creation in us it is not itself dependent on circumstances, though our openness to receive it may be conditioned by them. The pollution of external noise is a real problem in our world; we must do all in our power to find public solutions and to ensure adequate quiet for individuals, at least in patches. Nevertheless you can in a real sense absorb a good deal of noise, fuss and rush into yourself and transform it into quiet by the power of your peace. Conversely, you can by losing your peace generate more noise, fuss and worry. Like busyness,[6] noise can be part of your experience of the desert in situations where you cannot escape it and are prepared to believe in the lordship of Christ precisely here. This awareness of your power to receive his peace and be at peace in adverse circumstances is both a condition for prayer and a fruit of it.

Anyone who prays comes to grips with the problem of another kind of noise, the volatility of mind and imagination. We know we need inner silence if we are to listen to God; and when we have reached a stage in the relationship where our own thoughts about him or words to him seem like useless clutter in the time of prayer, we long to obey his invitation: 'Be still and know that I am God.'[7] Yet we fail and fail again. Prayer can become an apparent take-over by powerful distractions, and we come away feeling dissatisfied and thoroughly humbled.

If this failure is not understood and rightly accepted it can become a source of guilt-feelings about prayer which block progress. We need to be clear about what inner silence is and is not. It is not vacuity or mental paralysis. The Creator has made us with our delicate suggestibility: some external stimulus evokes a memory or an imaginative picture, this hooks on to some other thought by the power of association and away we go. If it were not so, we should never widen the range of our understanding, never be open to new ideas, never have an inspiration, never be inventive or creative. He has made us with this marvellous equilibrium of sense and spirit, and it is the whole human person who goes to him in prayer. If we have done our honest best, and not withdrawn the intention of the will to give that time wholly to God, it has been prayer. The way forward is not self-reproach or pseudo-contrition for something we cannot help, but acceptance of the kind of prayer that God makes possible now. In this is peace and union with his will. 'Of course quiet is necessary for peace. But if God does not wish us to have peace, we must be satisfied with confusion, and that *is* peace, of an elusive kind.'[8]

But of course this presupposes that we have done what we can to keep intellect and imagination quiet, for some measure of control can be achieved. It may help to repeat gently some word or short invocation: *The Cloud of Unknowing* recommends a one-syllable word like 'God' or 'Love'; Abbot Chapman mentions the use of some phrase like 'My God, I want you and I don't want anything else'. These are not the prayer itself; they are a sop to the imagination, something to keep it ticking over quietly while the higher intellect and the will engage in the real business at a level we cannot directly perceive, in the 'naked intent unto God'.[9] Distractions, provided they are not willed, do not matter now in the way they used to matter in meditation; they may flit across the surface but are best ignored. To worry about them, and to turn the will away from clinging to God in order to deal directly with them, is to abandon the real prayer. The author of *The Cloud* advises us to look over their shoulders;[10] there are other analogies too, like being with someone you love and being so intent on that person that you refuse to turn your attention away to swat a mosquito or answer the phone.

The real inner silence before God is a peaceful, total

acceptance of your being from him. It is more a matter of receiving his gift than of strained effort on your part. God himself is silent because he will not force himself upon you; your delicate freedom is too precious to him, and there is a devastating humility in his love. In your openness to him, beyond thoughts, words, and fragmented desires, your poverty meets his giving in the silence of lovers. In your deepest 'self'—not the empirical self of daily affairs but the ultimate truth of your being—you wait, trust, and consent to be loved. He has created your central stillness, and by his grace you have found your way into it.

Even in the world around us there are different kinds of silence. The silence of death or of not-yet-life, like that of the pre-Cambrian earth or the desert, is very different from the life-bearing, silent expectancy of winter for spring, or the silence of waiting for God. St Mark evokes it: 'as if a man should scatter seed upon the ground, and should sleep and rise night and day, and the seed should sprout and grow, he knows not how ...'[11]

Christ's Easter mystery is concerned with emptiness and fullness. In him the whole fullness of deity dwelt bodily,[12] yet he emptied himself and became obedient even to death. He invites us to go with him. We are promised that we shall be 'filled with all the fullness of God',[13] but only if we are willing to lose our life in order to find it. In prayer we consent to poverty and renunciation in a particularly direct way. We are asked to loose our hold on unreality, on the pseudo-self with its illusions and its cravings, and to *be* before God in the simple nakedness of faith. The more we have clung to some image of ourselves or to some function we fulfil as though that were what gave us meaning, the harder it will be to make this act of trust. All loving is a leap beyond our securities, and when God asks us to let go of everything that might seem to give us value other than his love alone, it is a very daring leap. In our hearts we long for this radical simplicity, but the emptiness can frighten us and tempt us to turn back. This is part of the point about distractions in prayer. They seem to promise life, while prayer is boring and empty and a losing of our ego-life. If we grab at them and follow them we are refusing to be poor and seeking to 'save our life', but helplessness in the grip of involuntary distractions while the will stands firm is a real poverty of spirit.[14]

Prayer springs from God's life in us. The living God who gives that life himself undertakes the pruning needed for its increase; he prunes through the experience of prayer and the diminishments we suffer in our lives. But he is at work on an intelligent creature whose co-operation is expected. Judicious pruning on your part may therefore also be required, the kind of 'No' to self that will give freer play to life and love. If you give yourself seriously to prayer you will know automatically when something is blocking you and holding you back from God. No elaborate examination of conscience is needed, for it leaps to the eye. It is not your frailties and failures that block, nor your limitations, but anything you hold on to when you know God wants you to let go of it. This is an obvious area for asceticism, though it may also be an area where healing is needed first before you can be free enough to let go.

Asceticism is not profitable if it is an attempt to justify your existence, if it closes you in on yourself, makes you conspicuous or complacent, damages health, builds up strain, interferes with duties, makes you less available for persons or for prayer or deprives you of the power to enjoy life. The criteria for necessary self-denial are love and wholeness. The useful 'No' is the kind that enables you to say 'Yes' to love whenever it calls you; the kind that makes you stand in the truth of your being in poverty of spirit before God, trusting and open to his mercy and fatherhood. This kind helps you to real solidarity with the have-nots of any variety, and at the same time frees you for an integrated body-spirit response to the beauty of creation. It opens you to abundant life. A great deal of asceticism is built into modern life for those living towards love and prayer and wholeness: the need to resist anxiety, rush, over-eating and the tyranny of advertising; the responsibility of deciding when enough is enough in a materialistic society; the call from God to use the good things of creation with care and respect.

Beyond this, asceticism is a matter of sensible strategy. Any worthwhile thing we do in life, and anything we really love, demands all we can give to it and therefore entails sacrifice. A professional sportsman or a concert musician accepts a very demanding programme of practice, the need for tremendous perseverance, disappointments, criticism and abstention from many other enriching activities. Yet he must look to the whole. To bring on a breakdown from overstrain is to defeat his end, so he looks to the end and chooses the means to it, allowing for judicious rest and holidays in order to get the best out of himself. This is part of the wisdom of the ages.[15]

Your prayer is your life, the worthwhile life that you know demands sacrifice if you are to give your best. You must also make enough room for it and this will be costly, perhaps entailing the renunciation or pruning of some activities that fill your leisure.[16] But all asceticisms are a means to an end, which is union with God, and it is good strategy to ensure that your life is balanced and your body and mind in good form. Fresh air, a disciplined but comfortable posture and the environment for prayer that best suits your temperament are common sense means.

The pruning you endure, whether by consenting to God's action or by personal decisions made in sensitive response to his will, is for the sake of life. Holiness and wholeness coincide in the end. What you are asked to deny and renounce are the things that militate against ultimate wholeness, the forces of unreality, anti-life and sin. You are promised all fullness, and in prayer you are gradually hollowed out to become more *capax Dei*, as the old writers used to say, more able to receive God. John of the Cross, the saint who advised those at the foot of the mountain, 'In order to possess all, seek to possess nothing', said in his mature holiness,

Mine are the heavens and mine is the earth; mine are the people, the righteous are mine and mine are the sinners;

the angels are mine and the Mother of God, and all things are mine; and God himself is mine and for me, for Christ is mine and all for me. What, then, dost thou ask for and seek, my soul? Thine is all this, and it is all for thee.[17]

There is so much love and joy even now; there are times when you can only be like the earth in the rain, drinking it in and letting it happen. Yet 'fulfilment', like happiness, is never found by being sought for its own sake. It comes from aiming off-target, just as in order to see a faint star at night you must not look directly at it. Nor will fulfilment be wholly found this side of death. The earth is given to us and we must glory in it, but it is not our home.

Love bade me welcome; yet my soul drew back,
    Guilty of dust and sin.
But quick-eyed Love, observing me grow slack
    From my first entrance in,
Drew nearer to me, sweetly questioning,
    If I lacked anything.

'A guest', I answered, 'worthy to be here.'
    Love said, 'You shall be he.'
'I, the unkind, ungrateful? Ah, my dear,
    I cannot look on thee.'
Love took my hand, and smiling did reply,
    'Who made the eyes but I?'

'Truth, Lord, but I have marred them; let my shame
    Go where it doth deserve.'
'And know you not', says Love, 'who bore the blame?'
    'My dear, then I will serve.'
'You must sit down', says Love, 'and taste my meat.'
    So I did sit and eat.[1]

One of the reasons why the Old and New Testaments speak a good deal about light is that God's people is always going somewhere, and needs it to travel by. The imagery of 'the way' is common to a number of the great world religions, but for those who are sons of Abraham by faith it is strengthened by historical memories. 'By faith [Abraham] sojourned in the land of promise, as in a foreign land, living in tents . . . For he looked forward to the city which has foundations, whose builder and maker is God.'[2] We shall not find here the fullness of union we are promised, either in prayer or in life, for 'here we have no lasting city, but we seek the city which is to come'.[3]

A fourteenth-century English writer told a parable about a pilgrim who wished to go to Jerusalem, but did not know the way. He asked another man, who warned him of the hard, long road and the dangers that beset it. The pilgrim replied that as long as he arrived there alive he did not mind how rough the going might be, so the other instructed him: 'Keep on your way and have no aim but to be at Jerusalem, for that is what you desire and nothing but that. And if you are robbed, or beaten, or treated with contempt, do not resist.... Put up with the harm you suffer and continue as though nothing had happened, lest you should suffer greater harm. And if men wish to keep you by telling you false tales to amuse you and turn you from your pilgrimage, do not listen and do not reply to them, but only say that you wish to be at Jerusalem. And if men offer you gifts and to make you rich with this world's goods, pay no heed to them, keep your mind always on Jerusalem. If you will keep to this way and do as I have said, I will answer for it that you will not be slain but that you will come to the place that you desire.'[4]

We do not, however, walk alone, nor is it only the saints, past and present, who bear us company. We go in the Easter Christ.

The idea of salvation as our return to God, our home-going after wandering, is strong in the New Testament. The sheep is found and carried back by a rejoicing shepherd; the prodigal goes back to his father. For both Paul and John the paschal mystery is Christ's own passage home. When Paul speaks of the redemption he habitually stresses two things. First, the passion was an act of love, obedience and freedom on Christ's part, not a succumbing to punishment; all the shame and pain that surrounded the cross were accepted freely and became an expression of love which transformed their meaning. Second, it is not by the cross alone that we are saved but by the single, indivisible mystery of his cross and resurrection; if Christ is not risen we are still in our sins. He has sought us in our far country, identified himself with us and drawn us by the strength of that identification into his Godward movement: 'God was in Christ reconciling the world to himself . . . For our sake he made him to be sin who knew no sin, so that in him we might become the righteousness of God.'[5] Our freedom and love are therefore also required, and our dignity thus respected. In union with his obedience we too can transform the suffering and the unsatisfactory conditions of our lives, and make them part of our passage home. The Father 'has delivered us from the dominion of darkness and transferred us to the kingdom of his beloved Son'.[6]

John's outlook is different, but the idea of Christ's passage and return to the Father is still clearer. The whole story is a downward, followed by an upward, sweep: 'I came from the Father and have come into the world; again, I am leaving the world and going to the Father.'[7] At the beginning of the last supper 'Jesus knew that his hour had come to depart out of this world to the Father'[8] and throughout John's gospel the 'lifting up' of Jesus always has the double sense: cross and exaltation to glory. Peter wants to go too, and is told that although he will have to wait, he will follow later.[9] Jesus intends to take his own with him: 'Father, I desire that they also, whom thou has given me, may be with me where I am.'[10] At the beginning of this gospel his first two disciples had asked Jesus where he lived, and had received the answer, 'Come and see'.[11]

So the prodigal son is not only this or that individual sinner repenting; he is our race returning to the Father incorporate in the beloved Son. Christ goes not limping and ashamed but with a rush of love and joy (like the boy on the roof). How this can be true for us as well is difficult to understand and still more difficult to put into words. If we believe that the love we are to encounter face to face at the end is enfolding us now, is inviting us to let go in life and prayer and to give ourselves, is continually asking us to open our hearts and receive; if we believe that we are building our eternity now and that the quality of each person's building will be revealed by the fire which burns away all shoddy work,[12] then it is hard to see how any of us will be able to meet God without shame. The poem by George Herbert at the beginning of this chapter evokes it finely. There is no difficulty about believing that Love will forgive us and bid us sit down at his banquet; the difficulty lies in understanding how we could have no regrets for having let him down: for grace wasted, opportunities lost and frequent unresponsiveness to the love that would have done more in us here and now if we had let it have its way.

Somehow the Father's love is able to deal with this. He can not only forgive and purify, he can love us so creatively that our omissions and negligences are made good, and our use of time itself redeemed. He will see to it that we do not spend eternity kicking ourselves. He can cleanse our eyes by this loving until we see him, ourselves and others in his light.[13] We have dim intuitions of this now, because his love is spread about in his children and we sometimes catch a flash of his likeness, as when a child by some movement or tone of voice or smile suddenly reminds us of his father or mother. Most of us have met, at least once, such unselfish love in another human being that our failures do not matter; we feel simultaneously humbled, ennobled and changed. It is evoked in some of the great literature of the world, as by Dostoievsky in his description of Shatov's joy when his wife returns to him.[14] Our business is to expose ourselves to it now in prayer, habitually if confusedly, knowing that 'when he appears we shall be like him, for we shall see him as he is'.[15]

Gloria Dei vivens homo, vita autem hominis visio Dei, said St Irenaeus in the second century: the glory of God is that man should be truly alive, and man is alive when he sees God. We are made for this. For the time being 'we see in a mirror dimly, but then face to face. Now I know in part; then I shall understand fully, even as I have been fully understood.'[16] The glory, the transforming vision, is very near to us, because we are touching the reality through faith and love. But we are still in darkness and cannot see it, like Mary Magdalene at the tomb.

'Contemplative' prayer is this nearness in the dark, at any rate in its early stages. The term 'contemplative' has been for the most part avoided in this book, because it is apt to mislead by suggesting clear vision or apprehension by the intelligence. The prayer beyond 'meditation' (that is, beyond acts of the will immediately prompted by the use of reason and imagination) is much more a matter of unseeing, much more a cleaving to God in trust and love, a 'loving stirring and blind beholding unto the naked being of God himself only'.[17] Blessed are the pure of heart, for they will see God, face to face in light one day, but here and now in this unknowing, in the night. Purity of heart is not smug innocence, but poverty of spirit, compunction, emptiness, bankruptcy and confidence, forgiven-ness and healed-ness.

St Paul has many things to say about prayer, but the best thing he says is that we cannot pray. We cannot, but the Spirit takes over: 'The Spirit helps us in our weakness; for we do not know how to pray as we ought, but the Spirit himself intercedes for us with sighs too deep for words. And he who searches the hearts of men knows what is the mind of the Spirit, because the Spirit intercedes for the saints according to the will of God.'[18] This is an astonishing statement, because the Spirit is God himself. Paul is apparently saying that God prays in us. An Old Testament prophet lamented,

> Where are thy zeal and thy might?
> The yearning of thy heart and thy compassion
> are withheld from me.[19]

They are not withheld now. Prayer is this love-yearning of God in us. *He* yearns through *your* heart. You have to align yourself with his loving, consent to it and let it happen. To Julian of Norwich the Lord said, 'I am the ground of thy beseeching'.[20]

The medieval schoolmen spoke of 'Uncreated Grace'; this is technical language for the fact that grace means first and foremost not gifts from God, however wonderful, but God giving himself. 'In that day' (the new day of the resurrection), said Jesus, 'you will know that I am in my Father, and you in me, and I in you.'[21] His Easter mystery releases in us the Spirit who is the Father's turning to the Son and the

Son's to the Father, the Spirit who is God's self-giving and communication. This Spirit prays in us. It is hardly surprising that his activity is too deep not only for our words but for our perception.

Yet God does not mean it to be entirely hidden even now. Although the mind is dark and blank and nothing seems to happen in our prayer, we do 'know' at another level the 'love of Christ which surpasses knowledge'.[22] This knowledge is an experience, a knowledge of the heart. One of the Spirit's gifts is wisdom, which is a sensitive ability to 'taste', a purified responsiveness and attunement to the things of God. Traditional theology speaks of 'connaturality'; the believer endowed with wisdom has understanding or insight through his kinship with the mysteries of faith. The gift of wisdom is found at full strength in Christian mystics, who are not some secret in-group but people who live experientially on the realities which are the birthright of every believer. The Spirit who searches the depths of God is given to us that we may know our new being in grace, which is our new being in God, and rejoice in it with him:

> 'What no eye has seen, nor ear heard,
> nor the heart of man conceived,
> what God has prepared for those who love him,'

> God has revealed to us through the Spirit. For the Spirit searches everything, even the depths of God. . . . Now we have received . . . the Spirit which is from God, that we might understand the gifts bestowed on us by God.[23]

With the psalmist, but beyond the range of his guessing, we can say, 'I thank you for the wonder of my being'.[24]

The Spirit's work is concerned with the whole man, because every dimension of our being is re-created in the Easter Christ. 'If the Spirit of him who raised Jesus from the dead dwells in you, he who raised Christ Jesus from the dead will give life to your mortal bodies also.'[25] As Christ's resurrection is a birth, so also is ours. He is the *first*-born from the dead, and many are to follow. The Church has traditionally called the death-day of the martyrs their *natalis*, their birth-day into heaven. By extension the same is true of all Christians: the martyrs have fellowship with the paschal Christ in a privileged way, but we are all called to follow. The present life is our ante-natal period, and ante-natal life is characterized by darkness, limitation and growth. We are being shaped for the fuller, freer life, when vision will succeed to darkness, but meanwhile we labour and suffer towards our new birth. The experience of pain, failure and limitation are necessary for the growth of the new life. 'Though our outer nature is wasting away, our inner nature is being renewed every day. For this slight momentary affliction is preparing us for an eternal weight of glory beyond all comparison, because we look not to the things that are seen but to the things that are unseen; for the things that are seen are transient, but the things that are unseen are eternal.'[26]

Not only are our bodies involved, but also the cosmos to which they inextricably belong. Contemporary man has good reason to be aware that the earth is shaped and loved or spoilt by the forces at work in the human heart. The earth too is marked for glory, through the passion and glory of man: 'Creation waits with eager longing for the revealing of the sons of God . . . because the creation itself will be set free from its bondage to decay and obtain the glorious liberty of the children of God. We know that the whole creation has been groaning in travail together until now; and not only the creation, but we ourselves, who have the first-fruits of the Spirit, groan inwardly as we wait for adoption as sons, the redemption of our bodies.'[27]

We can degrade things and tarnish joy by selfish grabbing and clinging. But as long as we do not cling to our joys, or to anything that we have experienced and celebrated, they stay pure and are immortalized in us. The resurrection will be the glorification and release not simply of your body but of everything in creation that you have enjoyed, experienced, loved and honoured through your body. Because all this has become part of you it will rise in you. And your rich, beautiful experience of life will be only an atom in the joy and experience of all mankind, in the whole search for truth, the moments of aching beauty that escaped and seemed to perish, the love that seemed to be wasted. Yet all this is only a tiny sharing in the creative joy of God.

Only through prayer can we grow free enough not to cling, and in prayer we pledge ourselves and all the human commonwealth to this joy, and let it abound. There is pain and there is cost, but none of it matters beside the joy; it is like the winning boat crew who, after sweating for four miles and expending more energy than the losers, can dance for joy at the finish; like the woman who no longer remembers the pain for joy that a child is born into the world; like the married couple still deeply in love after fifty years who will say that they would not have missed anything in the long, hard experience because all of it is an enrichment of the joy.

The grain of wheat, Christ dead and risen, is sown now in the earth of our still mortal bodies; he is the golden seed of immortal life and the pledge that everything truly human and truly alive in us will rise in glory. To this we must say 'Yes' in our life and prayer.

We may be doing so in a more or less solitary fashion, because we are so built that we can get deeper into prayer in solitude. This, however, is an aspect of our ante-natal limitation. Even now we pray and intuit 'with all the saints',[28] and in heaven contemplation will be fully shared. With all selfishness overcome we shall rejoice with open-hearted freedom in the joy of everyone else, in the goodness and beauty of God received and communicated differently by each. There seems to be no reason why we should not expect to go on growing and discovering indefinitely, transparent to all truth, heirs to all beauty and drinking at the inexhaustible springs of joy.

He has immeasurable use for each thing that is made, that His love and splendour may flow forth like a strong river which has need of a great watercourse and fills alike the deep pools and the little crannies, that are filled equally and remain unequal; and when it has filled them brim full it flows over and makes new channels. We also have need beyond measure of all that He has made. Love me, my brothers, for I am infinitely necessary to you and for your delight I was made. Blessed be He!

He has no need at all of anything that is made. An eldil is not more needful to Him than a grain of the Dust: a peopled world no more needful than a world that is empty: but all needless alike, and what all add to Him is nothing. We also have no need of anything that is made. Love me, my brothers, for I am infinitely superfluous, and your love shall be like His, born neither of your need nor of my deserving, but a plain bounty. Blessed be He![29]

The New Testament refers to Christians as 'the saints'. In the end there is no middle course open to us; mediocrity is a temporary option only, and a very short-lived one. In heaven we shall all be contemplatives, living wholly on these realities which are our life now because God has so loved the world, and known to us now because God has let us know, though obscurely. Prayer is living and loving now in accordance with these facts.

Holiness is not our achievement. 'In this the love of God was made manifest among us, that God sent his only Son into the world, so that we might live through him. In this is love, not that we loved God, but that he loved us....'[30] To trust him to see the job through and to lead you through prayer to holiness, that is, to perfect love, is therefore not to seek some extraneous favour but to fall in with his will in the particular part of it that concerns you. He wanted it before you did.

> Who more can crave
> > Than thou hast done,
> > That gav'st a son
> To free a slave,
> > First made of nought,
> > With all since bought?[31]

This poem is an echo of the *Exsultet* [32] and of Paul's lyrical passage: 'If God is for us, who is against us? He who did not spare his own Son, but gave him up for us all, will he not also give us all things with him? ... Who shall separate us from the love of Christ? Shall tribulation, or distress, or persecution, or famine, or nakedness, or peril, or the sword? ... No, in all these things we are more than conquerors through him who loved us.'[33] Paul goes on with a further list of menaces that might seem to separate us from that love; conceived in first-century terms they may not sound too dangerous to us today, but we can probably draw up a list of our own: I am sure that neither death, nor life, nor strikes, nor rising prices, nor falling standards, nor anxiety over our teenagers, nor past sins, nor present failures, nor bafflement, nor my obtuseness about prayer, nor the fact that I began to want it so late after wasting years, nor the fact that there is still so much that needs healing ... 'nor anything else in all creation will be able to separate us from the love of God in Christ Jesus our Lord'.[34]

When God has invested so heavily in it, is it reasonable to suppose that he is going to let his project fail, or succeed for only a minority? And if he is not, you must take the consequences for life and for prayer. St Augustine may fittingly have the last word. He is talking about martyrdom, but his remarks are applicable to all who walk in the Easter Christ along the road of prayer:

If we long ardently to arrive at that great good, we need have no fear of the rough journey. He who has promised is true, he who has promised is faithful, and in promising he cannot deceive us. Let us say to him then in all honesty, 'Because of your word I kept my feet firmly in your paths; there was no faltering in my steps'. Why are you afraid of those paths through suffering and tribulation? He has trodden them himself. 'But after all, he was Christ!' you may say. Well, the apostles went that way too. And still you argue, 'But they were the apostles!' All right then, but answer me: did not many other men tread the same path after them? And did not women tread it too?

97

Have you come to it well on in years? Then you should not be afraid of losing your life, for you are close to death in any case. Or have you come as a youth? Many young people, people who had life and its promises before them, have travelled along this way.... How can the track still be so rough, when such crowds have worn it smooth with their feet?[35]

Appendix: On Methods

This book has deliberately avoided any lengthy discussion of methods or techniques of prayer. It has been more concerned with prayer as a *life*, with the springs of that life in the scriptures, and especially with the various ways in which anyone who faithfully prays is led into Christ's paschal mystery. Nevertheless, some readers may be helped by brief indications of different ways into prayer, and some good books on each.

'Meditation', in the strict sense, means the use of our reason and imagination on the things of God. This naturally prompts a response in the will. These acts of the will may be of love, contrition, adoration, trust, thankfulness or anything else that is appropriate before God. Informal meditation can go on at any time of day or night whenever we are reminded of God, but in the time of prayer many people, especially Westerners, make it a more businesslike activity.

There are various methods. Some people begin from the gospels, selecting some passage that lifts them, perhaps imaginatively identifying with Peter, or Mary Magdalene, or a blind man, or a leper. This is a means to confrontation with Christ and his love that leads naturally into personal communion with him. Others prefer to use some form of words, such as the *Our Father* or a favourite psalm, saying a few words at a time and dwelling on each phrase as long as it continues to yield profit. Others again find it easier to begin from some vivid experience of their own which has been a revelation of God to them; it may be an experience of human love, of friendship, of beauty, or of one's own weakness and need of mercy.

The important thing to remember is that all these techniques are not prayer but launching pads, or ways of tuning in. The personal communion with God that flows from them is the prayer. It is therefore essential that we listen as well as speaking.

Sooner or later, however, a crisis occurs in the prayer of many people who have been meditating in some such way. It goes dead on them, and the experience is highly distressing. When it is the result neither of deliberate resistance to God's will nor of physical or psychological indisposition, this crisis may be one of growth. The person is being invited to a simpler kind of prayer, in which particular ideas and acts give way to a general, peaceful attention to God. The will is engaged with him, but the ordinary rational activity of the mind gets in the way if we try to use it as a means to prayer. At other times of the day we can still 'meditate', think, and use our minds on the things of God as well as ever. But this activity now seems to be incompatible with prayer.

The signs that the time has come to make the transition to simpler, imageless prayer are given in three places by St John of the Cross (*The Ascent of Mount Carmel*, Book II, Chapter 13; *The Dark Night of the Soul*, Book I, Chapter 9; *The Living Flame of Love*, Second Redaction, Stanza III, paragraph 34 ff.). A person finds it impossible to meditate at prayer, derives no pleasure from using the imagination on the things of God or on anything else, is painfully anxious about whether he is pleasing God (which shows that he is not simply lukewarm or careless about it all), and, especially, longs to be alone with God, lovingly waiting on him in silence.

This time of darkness, bewilderment and closeness to an unfelt God is what St John of the Cross calls the Night of the Senses. It is the entrance to contemplative prayer and the necessary preparation for further stages in which God will more and more take over as the human spirit yields to him. We can only wait for God in unknowing, without any clear perception of him or warm feelings.

One of the best books for helping people through the transition has been quoted many times already: Dom John Chapman, *Spiritual Letters* (London and New York, Sheed & Ward, 1959). Its Appendix I ('Contemplative Prayer, A Few

Simple Rules') should be read first. The following may also be useful: B. C. Butler, *Prayer, An Adventure in Living* (London, Darton, Longman & Todd, 1961).

A different approach to prayer, more helpful to many people than formal meditation and very ancient in Christian tradition, is the Prayer of the Name. The ancient monks of Egypt were accustomed to repeat continually some short invocation like 'O God, come to my help'. Later, some formula containing the name of Jesus came to be preferred, and as the 'Jesus Prayer' it has been widely practised among Christians of the Orthodox Churches. The invocation may be simply 'Jesus', or, in the longer form more common in recent centuries, 'Lord Jesus Christ, Son of God, have mercy on me, a sinner'.

The Jesus Prayer is murmured almost incessantly, with the lips or in the mind, as a person goes about his daily work, walks, eats, drops off to sleep or wakes up in the night. It is a prayer for mercy, and a means of remaining aware of God below the level of surface distractions; it is like an incarnation of God's love in Christ within our ordinary circumstances. It quietens the roving mind and gathers our scattered powers. Gradually it becomes attuned to the bodily rhythms of heart-beat and breathing, until the person's whole being—mind and voice, spirit and senses, and therefore also the universe of which our bodies are a part—is taken up into prayer. The practice of the Jesus Prayer leads into the 'prayer of the heart' which is central to the contemplative traditions of the East. This is the prayer of the deepest 'self' of which the physical heart is a symbol, prayer at that level of our being which is usually overlaid by multifarious activities and preoccupations, and of which we may be scarcely conscious. In this 'self' God dwells, and there we shall meet him.

The best introduction to this way of prayer is the anonymous Russian classic, *The Way of a Pilgrim*, and its sequel, *The Pilgrim Continues his Way* (translated by R. M. French, published in one volume by the SPCK, London, 1965). This

illuminating story tells how a simple, uneducated man discovered through the Jesus Prayer the meaning of the gospel
command, 'Pray without ceasing'. Very helpful also is the
anonymous pamphlet, *On the Invocation of the Name of Jesus*, by
a Monk of the Eastern Church (London, The Fellowship of
St Alban and St Sergius, 1970).

A Christian who by this means finds his way to his own
deep centre and meets God there, beyond all words and
images, experiences the 'awakening' which is the goal of
Indian mystical tradition. Indian sages have for many centuries recommended the use of a *mantra*, some short word
constantly murmured, as a means to pure self-awareness in
the centre of one's being. Much can be learned from Indian
wisdom by Christians on the road of contemplative prayer.
Two admirable books by a Christian steeped in Indian
tradition suggest the rapprochements: Swami Abhishik-
tananda: *Prayer* (London, SPCK, 1972) and *Saccidananda, A
Christian Approach to Advaitic Experience* (Delhi, ISPCK, 1974).

Notes

1 Letting Go

1 Phil. 3.7–12.

2 Phil. 3.13.

3 Cf. Mark 8.35; Matt. 10.39; Luke 17.33; John 12.25.

4 E.g. Mark 13.32; cf. Mark 6.6 (since surprise supposes antecedent ignorance). Possibly the memory of a mistake made by Jesus underlies Luke 2.41–52; he may have just realized at the human level that God was his Father, and thought this meant that he had to go and live in his Father's house. It was a child's reaction. But he accepted his mother's rebuke and went off with them to grow in wisdom, as well as in age and stature.

5 See Mark 8.33.

6 Luke 23.46.

7 Cf. John 17.11.

8 'Faith Unfaithful' by Siegfried Sassoon (1886–1967).

9 See John 19.30.

10 2 Cor. 5.14–15.

11 See Rom. 6.10–11.

12 John 1.14.

13 John 2.11.

14 See John 12.27–33; 17.1.

15 Phil. 2.5–11.

16 This too has a human reflection in the anguished but consenting love of Jesus's mother.

17 Cf. Ps. 139.

18 Easter Sequence in a St Gall MS, ninth–tenth century, English translation by Helen Waddell, included in *More Latin Lyrics, From Virgil to Milton* by Helen Waddell, edited by D. Felicitas Corrigan (Victor Gollancz 1976), pp. 331–2.

2 The Hidden Easter

1 Ps. 106.24. Throughout this book the psalms are quoted from the Grail Version, *The Psalms, Singing Version* (Collins, Fontana 1966), but the numbering of both psalms and verses of psalms is given according to the Hebrew, as in most modern Bibles. See a fuller note on this on p. 107 below (Note 3 to Chapter 6).

2   Mic. 6.8 (JB).
3   Ps. 25.14.
4   John 21.12.
5   Col. 3.3–4.
6   See Rev. 2.17.
7   See Luke 24.13–35.

3 *The Battle of Death and Life*

1   From an Easter Sequence.
2   Abbot Chapman's famous advice, 'Pray as you can, and don't try to pray as you can't', is worth remembering at every stage in the life of prayer.
3   An unpublished poem by Dom Philip Jebb.
4   Isa. 30.20–21.
5   Dom John Chapman, *Spiritual Letters* (London and New York, Sheed & Ward, 1959), p. 144.
6   Exod. 14.14.
7   Rev. 1.17–18.
8   Isa. 43.18–19.
9   See Deut. 30.19.
10 Heb. 10.31.
11 Mark 4.25.
12 John 10.10.
13 Isa. 49.9–10.
14 Ps. 84.6.
15 John 4.14; 7.37–9.
16 Ignatius, *Letter to the Romans*, vii.
17 See Ezek. 47.1–12.
18 Rev. 22.1–2.

4 *The Real Relationship*

1   Ancient Chinese poem, 'Cheng-tao Ke'; quoted by Alan Watts in *The Way of Zen* (Penguin Books 1962), pp. 164–5.
2   John 16.32.
3   Heb. 5.8.
4   See Mark 14.36 ('Abba'); for the address 'Father' see Matt. 11.25 and

Lukan parallel; Matt. 26.39, 42 and Lukan parallel; Luke 23.34, 46; John 11.41; 12.27, 28; 17.1, 5, 11, 21, 24, 25.

5 John 20.17.

6 Matt. 11.27.

7 See Col. 1.18; Rev. 1.5; Acts 13.33 (quoting Ps. 2.7 of the resurrection).

8 John 12.45.

9 To express the mutual indwelling and compenetration of the divine Persons the Greek Fathers used the word *perichōrēsis*, which evokes a circular dance. The Latins sometimes used the word *circumincessio*, 'a moving round in'. Other Latin writers, regrettably and unimaginatively, used *circuminsessio*, 'a sitting round in'.

10 'O happy fault!' The famous phrase occurs in the Easter hymn *Exsultet*:

What good would life have been to us
  had Christ not come as our Redeemer?

Father, how wonderful your care for us!
  How boundless your merciful love!
  To ransom a slave
  you gave away your Son.

O happy fault, O necessary sin of Adam,
  which gained for us so great a Redeemer!   (Trans. ICEL, Inc.).

11 Rom. 5.20–1.

12 *The Cloud of Unknowing*, by an anonymous fourteenth-century English writer, Chapter 40. The edition quoted in this book is that of Justin McCann (Burns & Oates 1952), but there are many..

13 See Luke 18.13–14.

14 John 18.37.

15 John 8.32.

16 'Burnt Norton' in *Collected Poems, 1909–1962* by T. S. Eliot (Faber and Faber 1963).

17 Hos. 11.8–9; Isa. 43.1; 49.15–16.

18 An old Indian sage is said to have advised people to think in terms of the cat-hold rather than the monkey-hold. A mother monkey transports her young from tree to tree on her back; the baby must cling tightly to his mother's fur or suffer the worst. But tigers and the other big cats carry their young in their mouths; the cub is held safely and cannot fall.

19 *The Stanbrook Abbey Hymnal*, revised edn, 1974, no. 10, p. 5.

20 Heb. 4.12–13.

21 Ps. 139.1–5, 7–10, 13–14.

5 *Freedom to Ask*

1   Heb. 7.16, 24, 25.

2   See Gen. 18.16–33.

3   See Num. 12.13.

4   See Exod. 32.11–14, 30–32; Num. 11.1–2; 14.13–20; 21.6–9.

5   See Exod. 17.8–12.

6   See Jer. 15.1; 2 Macc. 15.14.

7   See Isa. 42.1–9; 49.1–6; 50.4–11; 52.13—53.12.

8   See Isa. 53.10, 12.

9   1 Pet. 2.22.

10 1 Pet. 2.24.

11 Mark 10.45.

12 Luke 23.34.

13 He is also king, the fulfilment of the promises associated with David's dynasty. This is less relevant here, although the king was also a representative figure who on occasion offered sacrifice and interceded for the people; see 2 Sam. 6.17; 1 Kings 8.30–40.

14 Heb. 2.17–18; 4.15–16.

15 Rom. 8.33–4.

16 Col. 1.24.

17 See Heb. 12.1.

18 *Revelations of Divine Love*, Chs. 31, 32. The edition quoted in this book is that of James Walsh (Burns & Oates 1961), but there are many.

19 Op. cit., Ch. 5 and *passim*.

20 Luke 4.18.

21 See Mark 3.22–7.

22 Luke 13.16.

23 Mark 11.24.

24 John 14.12.

25 John 15.7; 16.24, 26–7.

26 See Mark 6.5.

27 The point was finely made by C.F.D. Moule: 'If we have reason to believe that the character of God is best seen in Jesus, and that the consistency of sheer moral perfection is the ultimate consistency, then we may have to revise our ideas of what is and is not "possible". And if we have reason to find in Jesus a unique degree of unity with the will of God, what is to prevent our believing that, where God is perfectly obeyed, there the mechanics of the material world look different from

what they do in a situation dislocated by disobedience? It is not that the regularities and consistencies are suspended or overridden; it is rather that our idea of how things work is based on too narrow a set of data. If the ultimate *locus* of consistency is in the realm of the personal—in the character of a God who "cannot deny himself"—then what is (in our present conditions) unusual need not be ultimately an intervention or an irruption or a dislocation or suspension of natural law; it need only be what "normally" happens—indeed what is bound to happen—on the rare and "abnormal" occasions when a right relationship is achieved in the family of God.' (*Miracles: Cambridge Studies in their Philosophy and History*, ed. by C.F.D. Moule (Mowbray 1965), 'Introduction' by C.F.D. Moule, pp. 16–17.)

28 Matt. 18.19–20.
29 See Matt. 6.7–8.
30 Julian of Norwich: op. cit., Ch. 6.

6 *The Prayer of the Psalms*

1 Hos. 11.1, 3.

2 Jewish tradition credited David with authorship of the psalms. This can no longer be maintained for all of them, although there is no reason to deny him an important role in initiating a movement of poetical and liturgical activity which continued for centuries. The problem of dating any particular psalm is complex, for during the whole period of its growth the psalter was a living, evolving thing. It is probable that the prayer of an individual was sometimes adapted for liturgical use; psalms originating in up-country sanctuaries were incorporated into the Jerusalem collections; royal psalms, bivalent from the outset, came to be used with explicit messianic reference after the exile; historical passages were re-interpreted in an eschatological sense.

3 A note on the numbering of the psalms: the Greek Septuagint version is out of step with the numbering of the Hebrew Bible throughout most of the psalter, because the Septuagint combines into one psalm the Hebrew Psalms 9 and 10 (calling it Psalm 9) and the Hebrew 114 and 115 (calling it Psalm 113); but the Septuagint separates into two the Hebrew Psalm 116 (calling it Psalms 114 and 115) and also the Hebrew Psalm 147 (calling it Psalms 146 and 147). The Authorized Version and most modern Bibles follow the Hebrew numbering. The Latin Vulgate and many liturgical books influenced by it follow the Greek. The correspondences are set out schematically below.

Hebrew	*Septuagint*	*Hebrew*	*Septuagint*
1–8	1–8	116.1–9	114
9	9.1–21	116.10–19	115
10	9.22–39	117–146	116–145
11–113	10–112	147.1–11	146
114	113.1–8	147.12–20	147
115	113.9–26	148–150	148–150.

4 Heb. 10.5–7; cf. Ps. 40.6–8.

5 Luke 9.51. The whole of this part of Luke's gospel (9.51–18.14) is cast in the form of a journey to Jerusalem; cf. Mark 10.34–35.

6 Luke 19.41–44; cf. 13.34–35.

7 See Mark 14.26. The 'Hallel' consisted of Pss. 113–118.

8 Ps. 41.9; John 13.18.

9 Ps. 69.4; John 15.25; cf. Ps. 35.19.

10 Mark 15.34.

11 Ps. 22.6–8.

12 Ps. 22.24.

13 Ps. 22.15–18 (the order of the lines is adjusted in the Grail version); cf. John 19.24.

14 Ps. 69.21; cf. Ps. 22.15; John 19.28.

15 Ps. 31.5; cf. Luke 23.46.

16 Luke 24.44–45.

17 Ps. 118.13, 15–17, 22.

18 Ps. 57.7–9.

19 Augustine, *Enarratio in Ps. lxxxv*, 1.

20 See John 2.19–22: '"Destroy this temple, and in three days I will raise it up".... But he spoke of the temple of his body.'

21 *Exsultet*, trans. ICEL, Inc.

22 There seems to be no reason why Christians who are not committed by their vocation to using the whole psalter should try to make all the psalms viable for prayer; they have a right to be selective. The problem is more acute for people whose vocation includes regular liturgical patterns of prayer that make use of the whole psalter; they have to come to terms in some way with psalms they would never personally choose as an expression of prayer. In addition to what is said in the text about psalms of violence, it is perhaps worth remarking that the sheer tedium of certain psalms need not be an insuperable

block. The experience of life is the raw material of prayer, and much of our lives too is routine, banal stuff.

23   Exod. 7–13.

24   Exod. 14.14; cf. 14.25, 'The Egyptians said, "Let us flee from before Israel; for the Lord fights for them against the Egyptians".'

25   Exod. 15.1 (Grail version). The blessed sing it in heaven, celebrating the Lamb's victory, according to Rev. 15.3–4.

26   See Dan. 7–12.

27   Ps. 24.8; John 12.31.

28   Ps. 109.1; 22.2; 83.1.

29   Ps. 42.1–2; 63.1.

30   Ps. 63 *passim*.

31   Ps. 130.6.

32   Ps. 131.1–2.

33   Ps. 17.8; 36.7; 61.4; 63.7; 91.4.

34   Ps. 63.8; 73.23.

35   Ps. 23.5; 36.8; 63.5.

36   Ps. 56.8.

37   Ps. 31.20.

38   Ps. 27.8–9.

39   Isa. 26.9, a psalm-like passage (unidentified version).

40   Ps. 46.10.

41   Ps. 25.5, 7, 9, 11, 16, 18.

42   Ps. 51.10–11, 17.

43   Ps. 31.12.

44   Ps. 30.7, 11.

45   Ps. 36.7–9.

46   Ps. 63.1.

47   Ps. 65.8–11.

48   Ps. 90.1–2.

49   Ps. 139.14–15.

50   Ps. 104.3, 10–12, 20–1.

51   Ps. 104.29–30.

7 *Creation*

1   From *The Stanbrook Abbey Hymnal*, revised edn, 1974, no. 44, p. 17.

2   Gen. 1.2.

3 Gen. 2.7; cf. Ps. 104.29; Gen. 3.19; Eccles. 3.20; 12.7; Job 34.14–15; 33.4.

4 Ezek. 37.1–14.

5 Judg. 3.10; 6.34; 11.29; 1 Sam. 11.6; Num. 11.17, 25–6; 2 Sam. 23.2; 2 Kings 2.9; etc.

6 Isa. 11.1–2; cf. 42.1–2.

7 Isa. 44.3.

8 Ezek. 11.18–20; 36.26–7; Joel 3.1–2; cf. Num. 11.29.

9 Luke 1.35.

10 Rom. 8.11.

11 Acts. 2.1–13; 1 Cor. 12.4–30.

12 E.g. the dinosaurs, which we are so ready to write off as a failed experiment on nature's part, dominated the scene for about a hundred million years, some twenty to thirty times as long as our species is so far known to have been here.

13 Exod. 33.18.

14 Exod. 33.20.

15 See Exod. 34.29–35.

16 See Gen. 32.24–32. This is a strange story and a very old one, probably the product of layer upon layer of tradition. It is possible that in earlier forms of it the adversary was not Yahweh but some local deity or demonic being who was really bent on blocking Jacob's entry into the promised land. But since the Yahwist writer revised and retained it, and linked it with the name of destiny, Israel, we are justified in reading it in the form given. As such it is open to a meaning that transcends a particular episode in Jacob's life. It expresses something of Israel's experience of God, and of ours: 'Israel has here presented its entire history with God almost prophetically as such a struggle until the breaking of the day' (G. von Rad, *Genesis* (S.C.M. Press, 2nd edn, 1963), p. 320).

17 See Exod. 20.4; Deut. 5.8.

18 Gen. 1.27.

19 Ps. 8.5–6.

20 Gen. 2.7.

21 Cf. John 1.3.

22 Col. 1.15–17.

23 1 Cor. 15.45, 47, 49.

24 Cf. note 7 to Ch. 7 above.

25 2 Cor. 4.4, 6–8, 10–11.

26 2 Cor. 3.18.

27 See Mark 9.4; Exod. 33.18–23, 11; 1 Kings 19.9 ff.

28 See Luke 9.31.

29 John 5.17.

30 See John 5.21–9.

31 See John 16.21–2. It has been pointed out by George Montague in *Riding the Wind* (Ann Arbor, Michigan, Word of Life, 1974), pp. 68–70, that in several gospel passages there are indications of a 'travailing prelude' to the healing word spoken by Jesus, a kind of little chaos before the creative act. Sometimes the disturbance is in Jesus himself: he groans before curing the deaf-mute (Mark 7.34) and is deeply troubled before the raising of Lazarus (John 11.33, 38). In other instances chaos is unleashed in other people or in the environment as he approaches: a demoniac shrieks and is convulsed (Mark 1.26); the pigs at Gerasa are stampeded by the cure of another demoniac (Mark 5.13); the epileptic boy falls into violent convulsions and foams at the mouth before his healing (Mark 9.20, 26). Jesus is Lord of the dark, chaotic areas in man. This means, further, that the chaotic areas in our own lives and work, and especially the chaos we are pleased to call our prayer, are not something that must be thrust out of his sight. Chaos is the preferred material over which Jesus breathes the re-creative Spirit, who can recycle it into praise.

32 John 20.20.

33 John 20.22–3.

34 Rev. 3.20.

35 Cf. Shakespeare's presentation of King Henry V's speech before Agincourt:

> He that shall live this day, and see old age,
> Will yearly on the vigil feast his neighbours,
> And say, 'Tomorrow is Saint Crispian.'
> Then will he strip his sleeve and show his scars,
> And say, 'These wounds I had on Crispin's day.'
>
> (*Henry V*, Act IV, Scene iii).

36 Cf. Julian of Norwich: op. cit., Ch. 39: 'After he [the lover of God] is healed, his wounds are still seen before God—yet not as wounds but as honourable scars.... In heaven we shall be rewarded by the courteous love of our God almighty, who desireth that none that come thither should lose any degree of their labour. For he seeth sin as sorrow and pain to his lovers; and to them he assigneth no blame, for love ... And so shall all shame be turned into worship and joy.'

37 There is an analogy here with the senses, which are our channels of communication with present reality outside ourselves. They can be channels of pain: we suffer through our sense of touch if we are cold or burnt, through hearing when exposed to cacophony, and so on. If we were desensitized we should not so suffer, but we should also be rendered incapable of a huge experience of life, of other people and of

God's self-revelation. Memory is the channel through which we have contact, individually and collectively, with past realities, and it too can be a channel of pain. But just as God means our sensuous life to be far more than a capacity for being hurt, so our memory is meant to be far more than a mass of wounds that need his healing. It has a positive job to do as part of our power to respond to him.

38 Cf. *De Trinitate*, Books viii–xv. Augustine was thinking as a Platonist: objects in the sensible world remind the soul of the ideal world which was its own original home, and thus all true knowledge is a 'remembering'. We need not accept all Augustine's Platonism to recognize the value and influence of his 'psychological' approach to the mystery of the Trinity.

39 On this see Ch. 6, 'The Prayer of the Psalms'.

8 *Towards Wholeness*

1 Clement of Alexandria, *Protreptikon*, 1.

2 Isa. 50.10.

3 John 9.25.

4 Mal. 4.2.

5 Luke 1.78 (JB).

6 See the fragment of a lost work *On Baptism* by Melito of Sardis, a second-century theologian, as quoted in Hugo Rahner, *Greek Myths and Christian Mystery* (Burns & Oates 1957), p. 115. Melito wrote: 'When drawn by his fiery steeds the sun has completed his daily course, then by reason of his whirling passage he takes on the colour of fire and becomes as a burning torch. When he has completed half his fiery journey, he appears so near to us that it is as if he would burn up the earth with his rays. Then, almost lost from view, he descends into the ocean. Now if we take a copper ball that is inwardly full of fire and radiates much light and plunge it into cold water, it hisses mightily but is made bright by the sheen of it, yet the fire within it is not extinguished but can blaze forth again and give a great light. So also is the sun; burning like the lightning, he is not extinguished when plunged into the cold water but keeps his fire alight without for a moment letting it die. Bathing himself in the mysterious depths he shouts mightily for joy, for water is his nourishment. He remains one and the same, yet he comes forth strengthened out of the depths, a new sun, and shines his light upon men. . . . And now he has made the darkness of night to flee away and brought us the shining day. There follow him in due course the dancing ranks of the stars and by reason of him the moon puts forth her power. They bathe in the baptistry of the sun like those who are obedient under instruction and it is only

because moon and stars follow the course of the sun that they shine with a truly pure light.... King of Heaven, prince of creation, sun of the eastern sky who appeared both to the dead in Hades and to mortals upon earth, he, the only true Helios, arose for us ...'
The present chapter is indebted to Rahner's book.

7   See Cyril of Jerusalem, *Catechesis to the Newly Baptized (Mystagogica* 1, PG 33.1069, 1073). This 'orientation' in prayer was common in early Christianity outside the baptismal liturgy. It probably had an eschatological significance at first, since Christ was expected to come from the east at his *parousia* (cf. Matt. 24.27), and so also to fetch the individual Christian, especially the martyr, at the hour of death by coming from the east.

8   G. K. Chesterton, *The Ballad of the White Horse*, Book ii.

9   Ps. 2.8.

10 George Mackay Brown, *Letters from Hamnavoe* (Edinburgh, Gordon Wright, 1975), p. 119. The author comments: 'There is some notion here of resurrection, we may be sure. ... They were poets in stone. Their bodies responded vividly to changes of light and darkness, in a way that those of television viewers don't. ...' And further: 'We cannot conceive how eagerly and anxiously those primitive Orkneymen brooded on the scales of summer and winter. After the harvest feast the tribe was fast caught up in the tides of darkness. The grass withered, the animals were butchered, the kindly life-giving sun swung in an ever-narrowing arc through the sky.... They could not tell whether the twenty-first or the twenty-second [of December] was darker. Orkney on both days was a cluster of cold shadows. Was there a faint subtraction of shadows on the twenty-third? They could not be sure.... By noon of the twenty-fourth there could be no doubt about it. The light was beginning to return to the world. They were on a tide that would bear them towards the first flowers, the birth of lambs, midsummer, the golden sheaf of corn. At midnight on the twenty-fourth of December ... there would have been wild rejoicing. The early Irish monks ... pointed out, gently, that indeed the promised Light of the World had come at Yule; the merest bud of light, a child in a poor stable in the east'. (Ibid., pp. 29–30.) To this book the passage about Maes Howe is indebted.

11 John 3.30.

12 Hilaire Belloc, Sonnet iii in *Sonnets and Verse* (Duckworth 1947), p. 5.

13 Christianity spread in the northern hemisphere before the southern, and this fact has evidently influenced its marriage with seasonal mysteries.

14 But on a derelict house in Hampstead there once appeared the splendid graffito: 'Remember, the fields sleep beneath.'

15 Gen. 8.22.

16 On all this see Hugo Rahner, *Man at Play* (Burns & Oates: Compass Books, 1965); and C. S. Lewis, *Voyage to Venus* (Pan Books 1953), pp. 198–202.

17 Cf. p. 29 above; the boy on the roof is not only Christ, he is also the *puer aeternus* and the spirit of play in yourself.

18 Prov. 8.27–31 (JB).

19 Ps. 104.25–6.

20 Job 39.19–21, 24–5; 40.15–18.

21 Baruch 3.34.

22 Laurens van der Post tells how when he pressed the Bushmen of the Kalahari to tell him their ideas about the beginning of things, one of them replied, 'It is very difficult, for always there is a dream dreaming us.' (*The Heart of the Hunter*, (The Hogarth Press 1961) p. 151).

9 *Pruning*

1 John 15.1–2, 5, 8.

2 Do you think this book came easily and all of a piece? Or that it can do its work properly without your creative and sympathetic reading?

3 See Gen. 32.24–32.

4 From 'Wrestling Jacob' by Charles Wesley (1707–1788).

5 John 14.27.

6 Cf. pp. 13–15 above.

7 Ps. 46.10.

8 Dom John Chapman, op. cit., p. 55.

9 See *The Cloud*, Ch. 3, also Chs. 39–40. See also Chapman, op. cit., especially pp. 57–61, 136, 287–94.

10 Op. cit., Ch. 32.

11 Mark 4.26–7.

12 Cf. Col. 2.9.

13 Eph. 3.19.

14 Cf. *The Cloud of Unknowing*, Ch. 32: 'When thou feelest that thou mayest in no wise put them down, cower then down under them as a caitiff and a coward overcome in battle, and think that it is but folly to strive any longer with them; and therefore thou yieldest thyself to God in the hands of thine enemies. . . . If this device be truly conceived, it is nought else but a true knowing and a feeling of thyself as thou art . . . the which knowing and feeling is meekness. And this meekness meriteth to have God himself mightily descending, to venge thee of thine enemies, so as to take thee up and cherishingly dry thy ghostly

eyes, as the father doth his child that is on the point to perish under the mouths of wild swine or mad biting bears.'

15   A story is told of Gautama Buddha and an enthusiastic young monk named Sona who paced up and down meditating until his feet bled, whereupon he was so discouraged that he was tempted to abandon the order. 'Now, Sona,' Gautama asked him, 'you were formerly a skilled lute player, were you not?' 'Yes, sir.' 'when the strings of your lute were tuned too tightly, could you get the right tune?' 'No, sir.' 'But if the lute strings were too slack, could you play well then?' 'No, sir.' 'So when the strings were neither too tight nor too slack, then the instrument was fit to play?' 'Yes, sir.' 'Just so. Too much zeal brings restlessness, but excessive slackness leads to mental sloth' (from the *Mahavagga Vinaya Pitaka*).

16   One can usually make time for what one really wants to do and considers important. The statement, 'I haven't time for X', is often translatable into 'X is not high enough on my list of priorities for me to be willing to make time for it'. One of Abbot Chapman's favourite maxims was 'The less you pray, the worse it goes'.

17   'Prayer of the Soul Enkindled with Love', printed after 'The Living Flame of Love' in *The Complete Works of Saint John of the Cross*, Vol. iii, translated and edited by E. Allison Peers, (Burns & Oates (three volumes in one), 1964), pp. 221–2.

10 *The End of the Beginning*

1   'Love' by George Herbert (1593–1633).

2   Heb. 11.9–10.

3   Heb. 13.14.

4   Walter Hilton, *The Scale of Perfection*, Book ii, Ch. 21, translated into Modern English by Dom Gerard Sitwell (Burns & Oates 1953).

5   2 Cor. 5.19, 21.

6   Col. 1.13.

7   John 16.28.

8   John 13.1.

9   Cf. John 13.36.

10   John 17.24.

11   John 1.39.

12   Cf. 1 Cor. 3.12–15. The value-judgments we form now about our achievements may have to be revised when death gives us new perspectives.

13   Cf. note 36 to Ch. 7 above.

14   See Dostoievsky, *The Devils*, Part 3, Ch. 5.

15 1 John 3.2.

16 1 Cor. 13.12.

17 *The Cloud of Unknowing*, Ch. 8.

18 Rom. 8.26–7.

19 Isa. 63.15. Admittedly he goes on in the next verse to call God our Father and Redeemer.

20 Julian of Norwich, op. cit., Ch. 41. Cf. ibid., Ch. 6: 'Our kindly will is to have God, and the good will of God is to have us. Nor may we ever cease willing or loving, until we have him in fullness of joy. And then we may no more will.'

21 John 14.20.

22 Eph. 3.19.

23 1 Cor. 2.9–10, 12.

24 Ps. 139.14.

25 Rom. 8.11.

26 2 Cor. 4.16–18.

27 Rom. 8.19, 21–3.

28 Cf. Eph. 3.18.

29 C. S. Lewis, *Voyage to Venus* (Pan Books 1953), p. 201.

30 1 John 4.9–10.

31 From 'A Hymn to God the Father' by Ben Jonson (1572–1637).

32 Cf. note 10 to Ch. 4 above.

33 Rom. 8.31–2, 35, 37.

34 Cf Rom. 8.39.

35 Augustine, *Sermo 306, In Natali Martyrum Massae Candidatae*, Ch. 11.